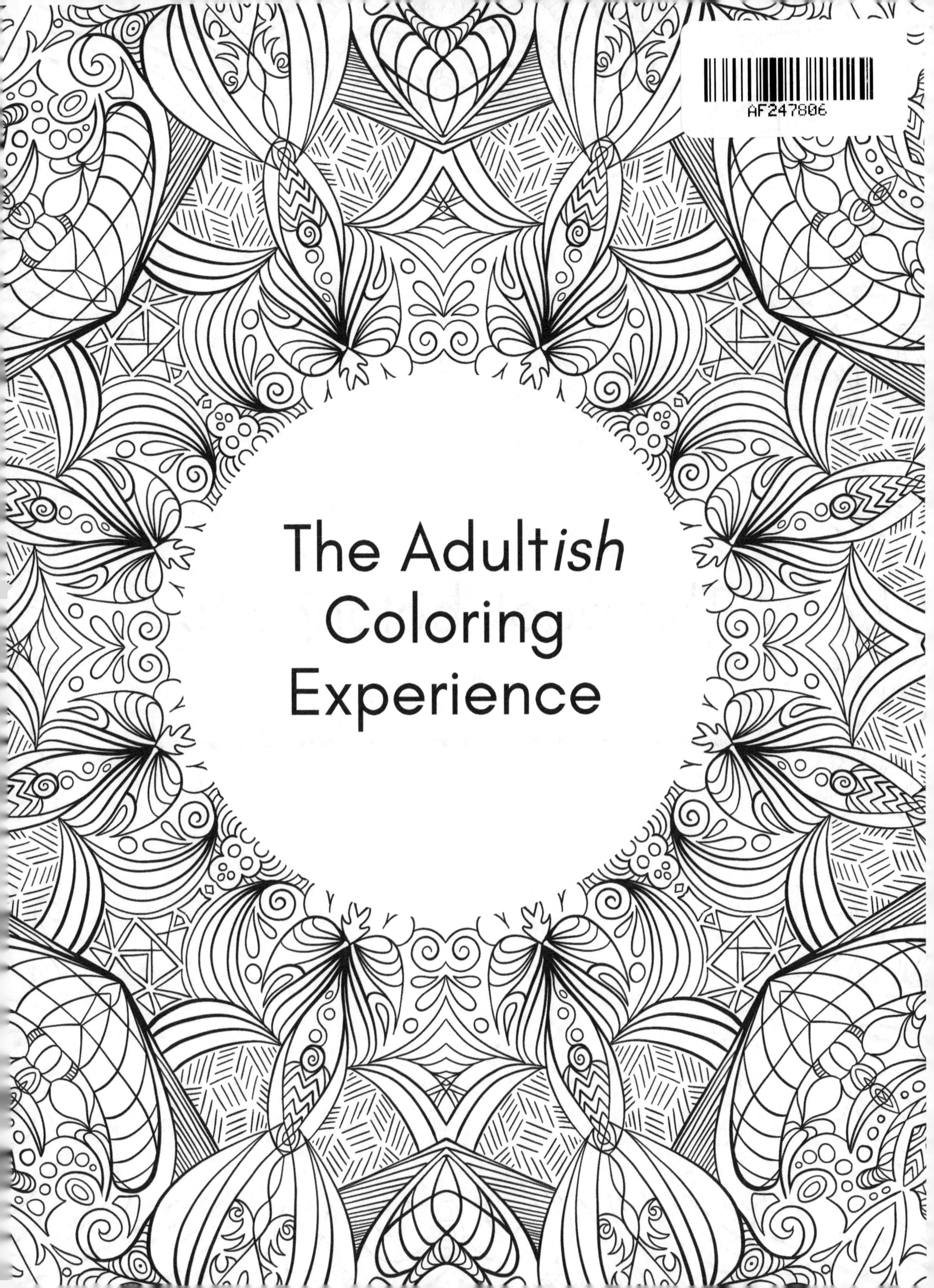

The Adultish
Coloring
Experience

This book belongs to

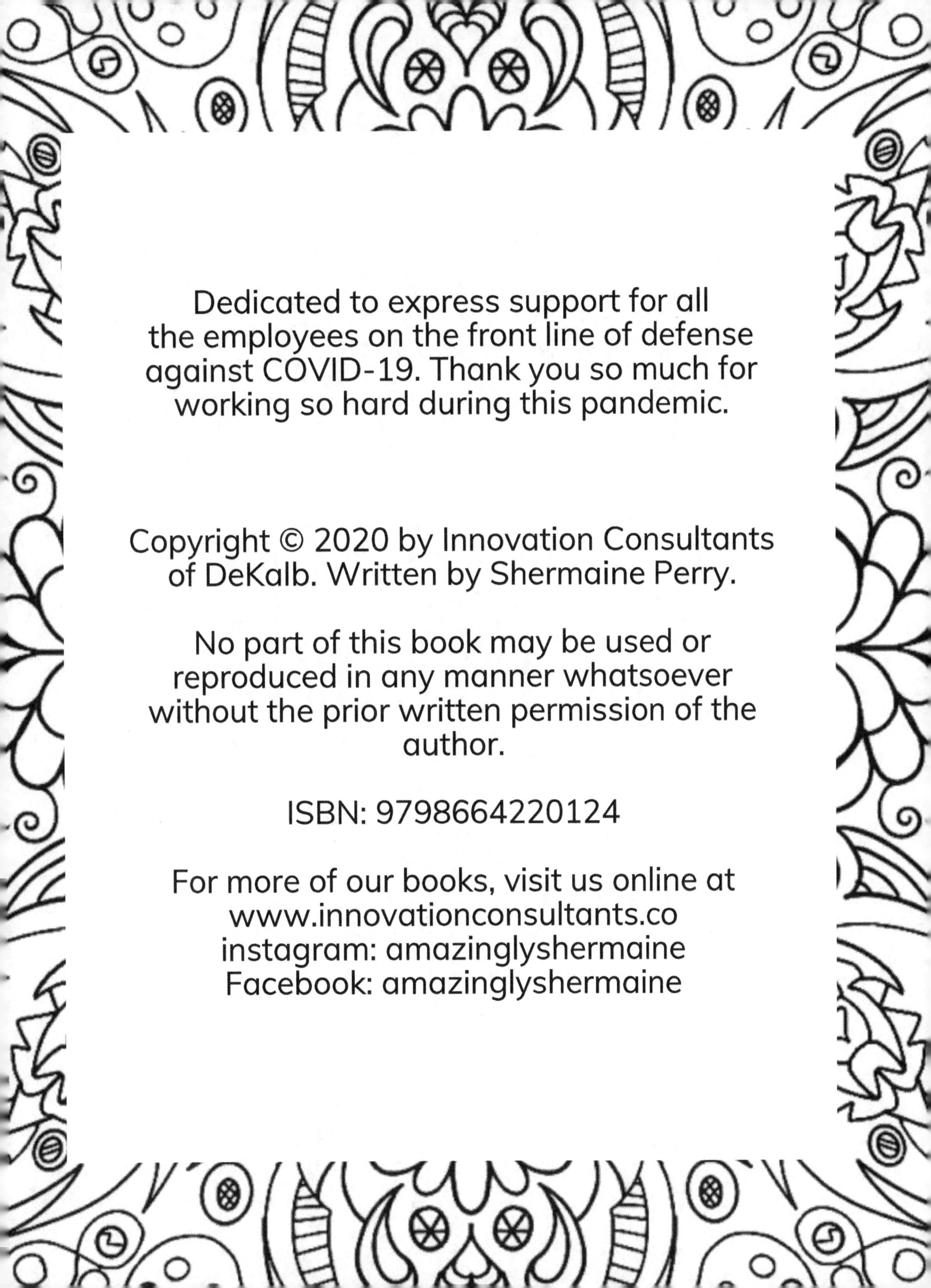

Dedicated to express support for all the employees on the front line of defense against COVID-19. Thank you so much for working so hard during this pandemic.

For more of our books, visit us online at
www.innovationconsultants.co
instagram: amazinglyshermaine
Facebook: amazinglyshermaine

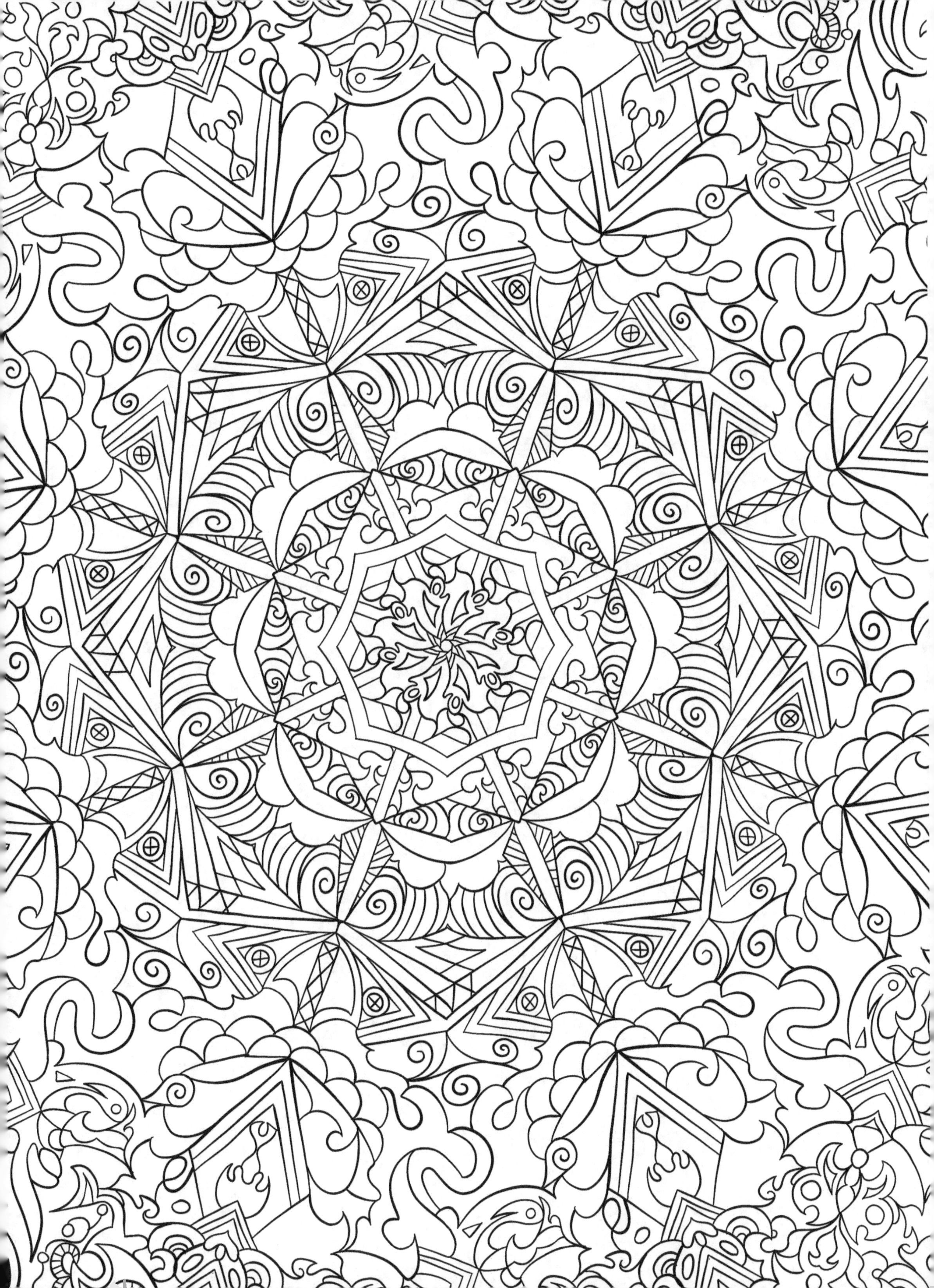

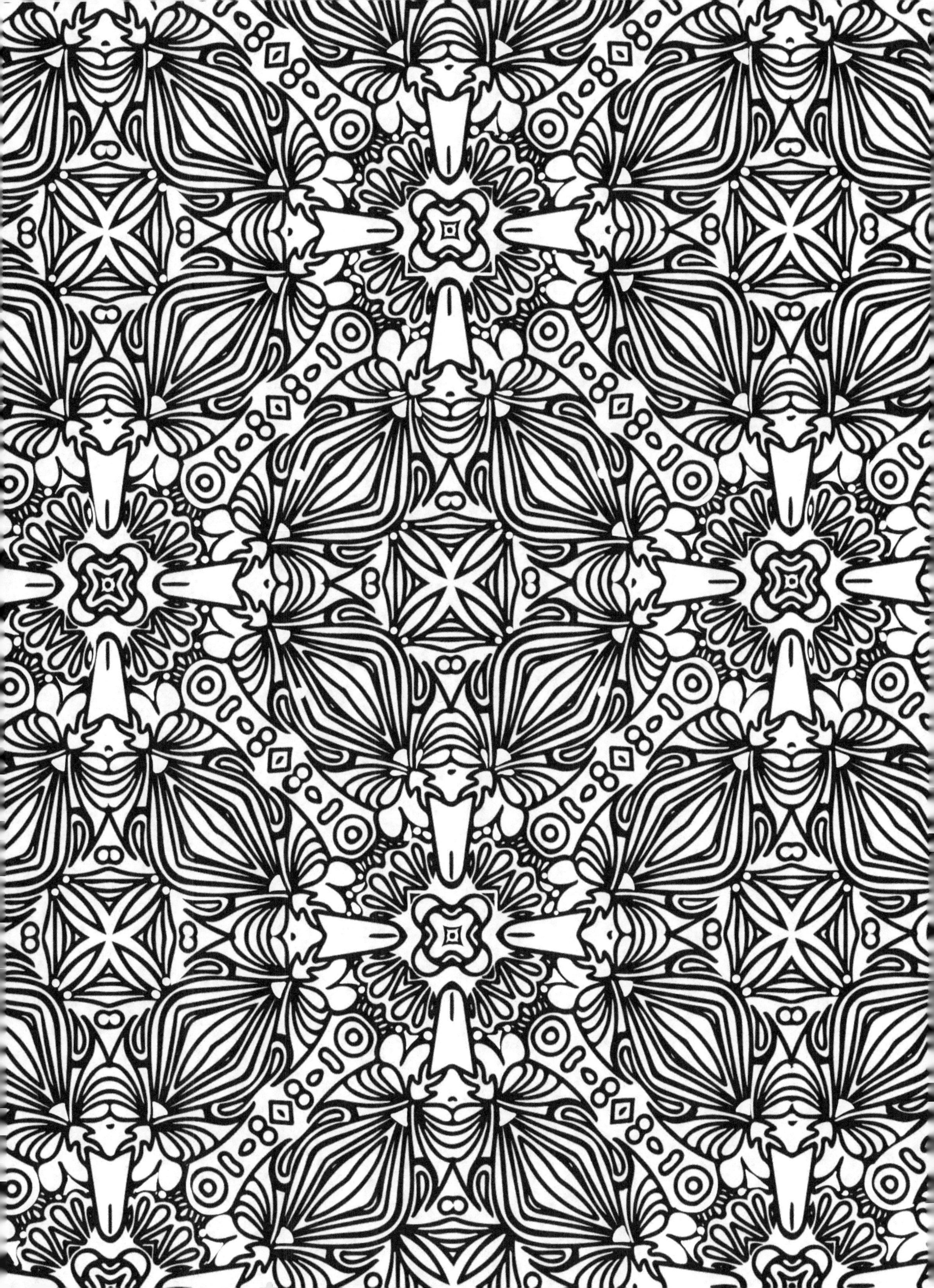

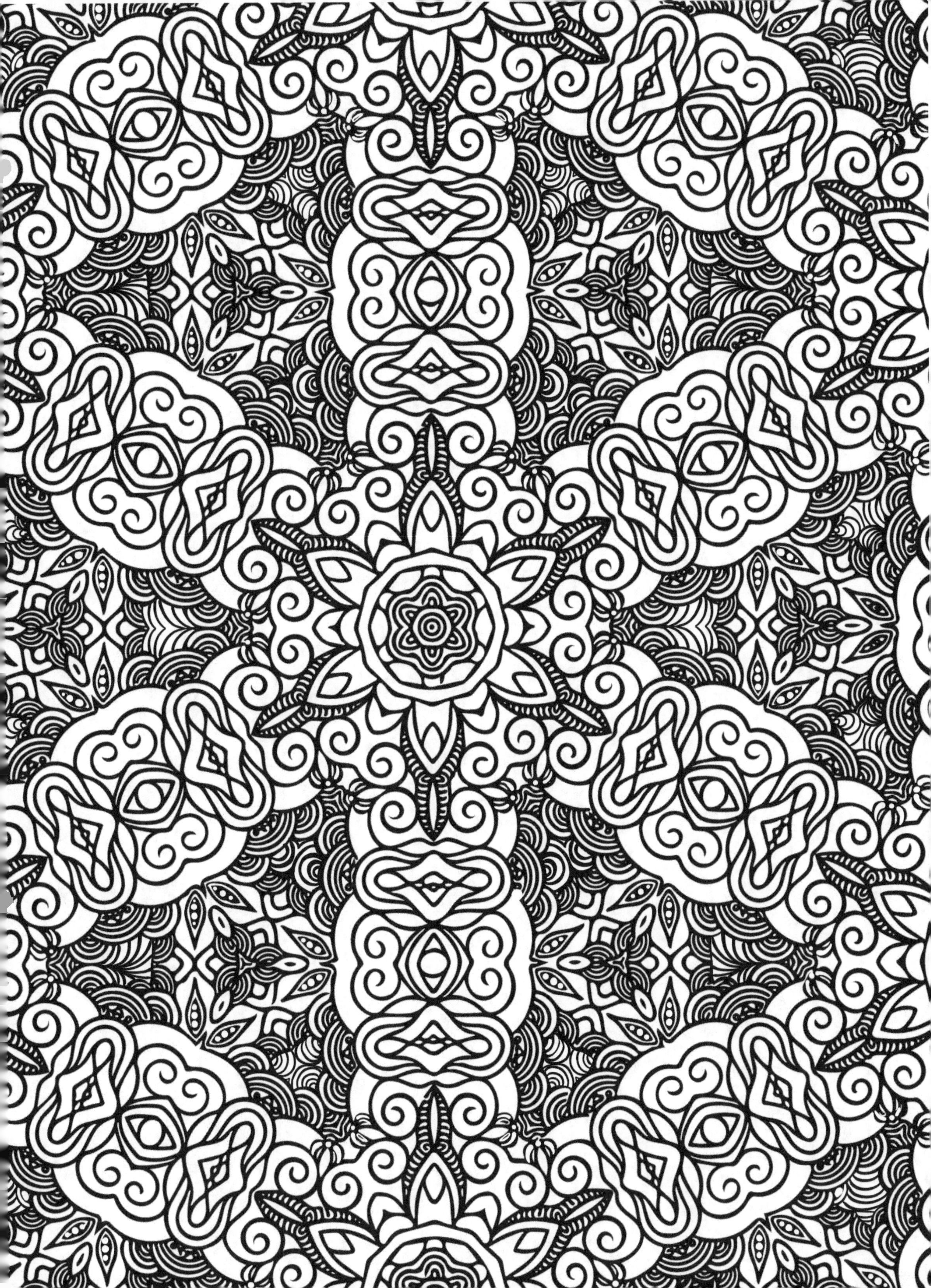

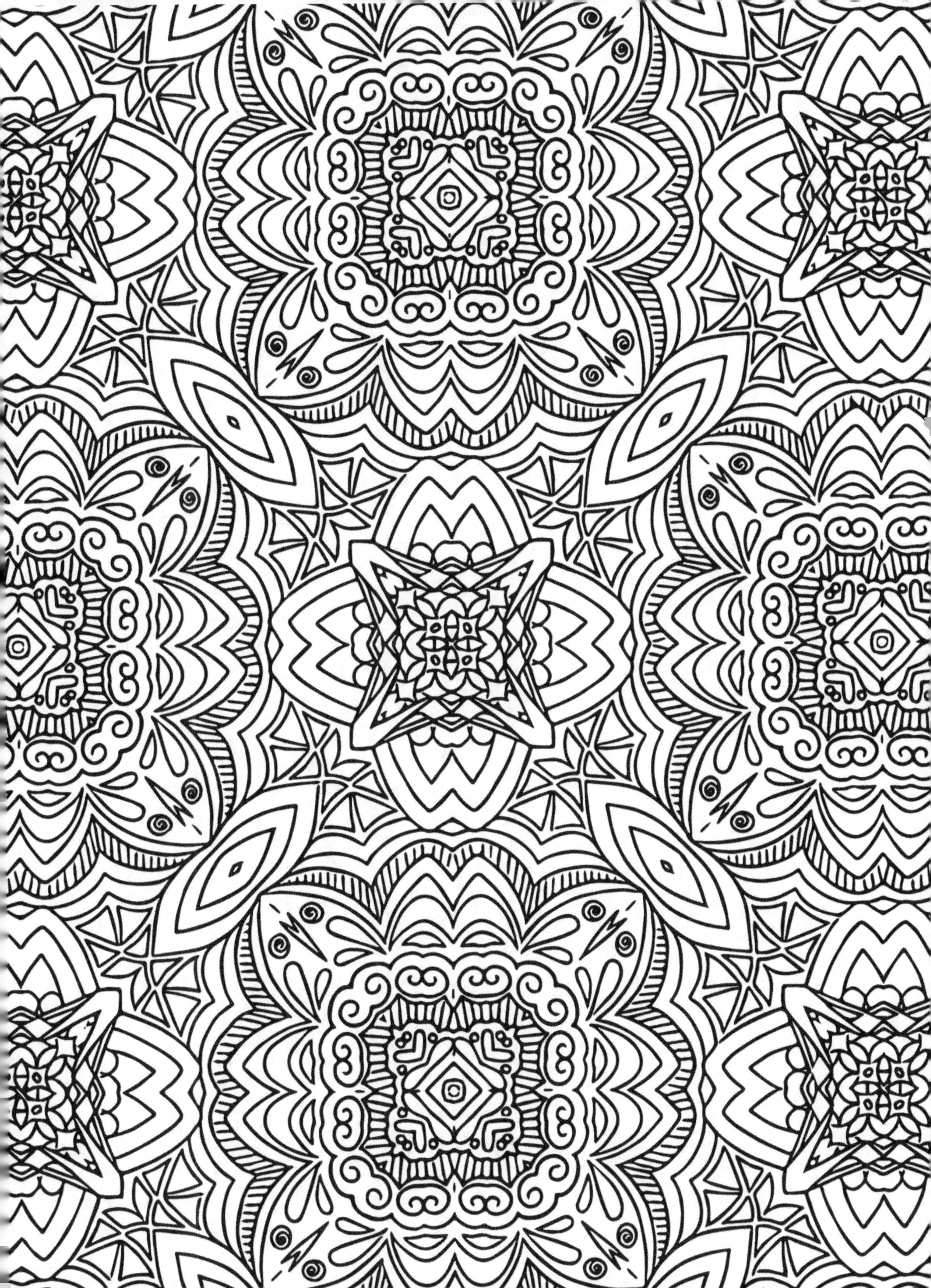

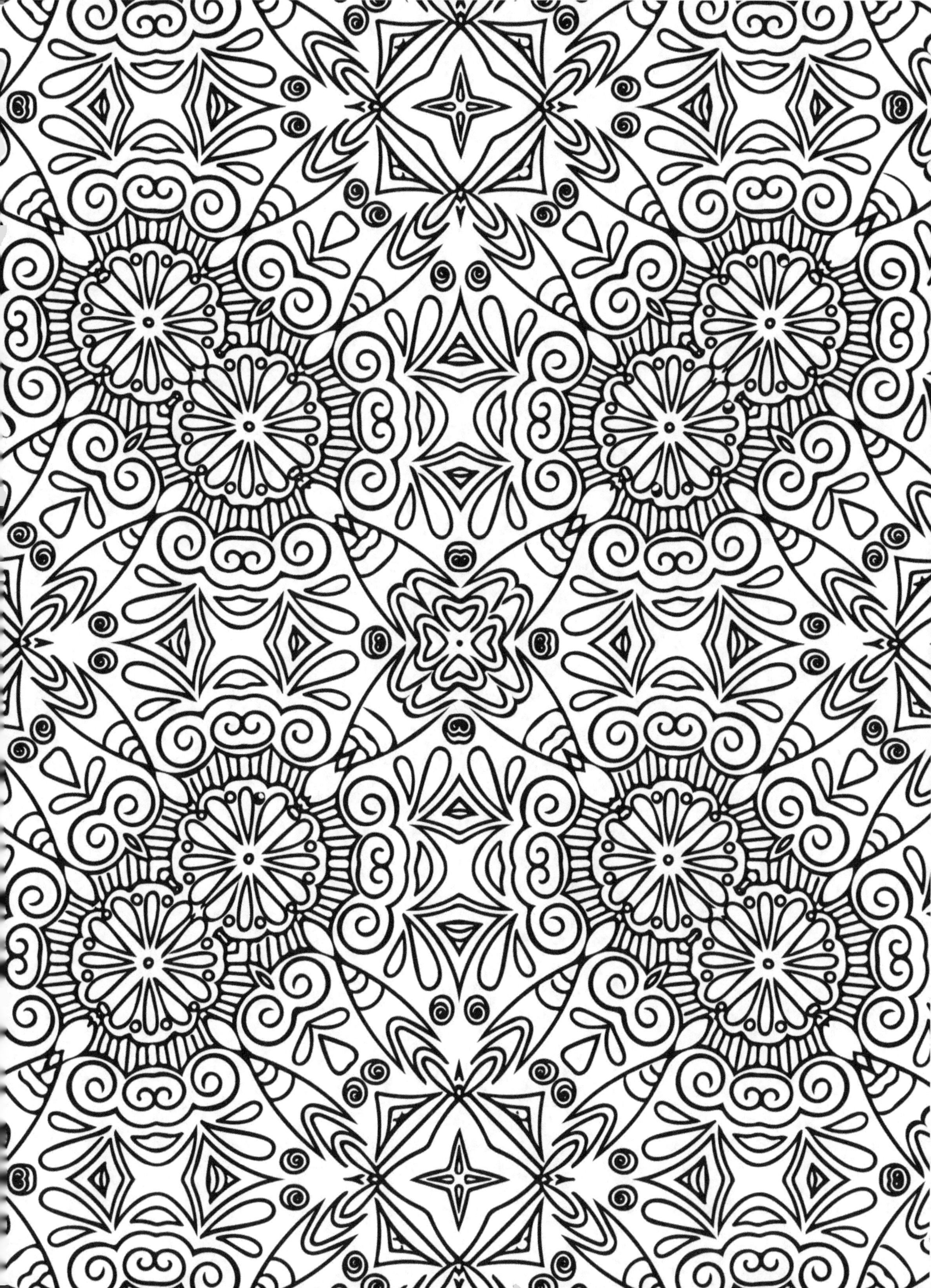

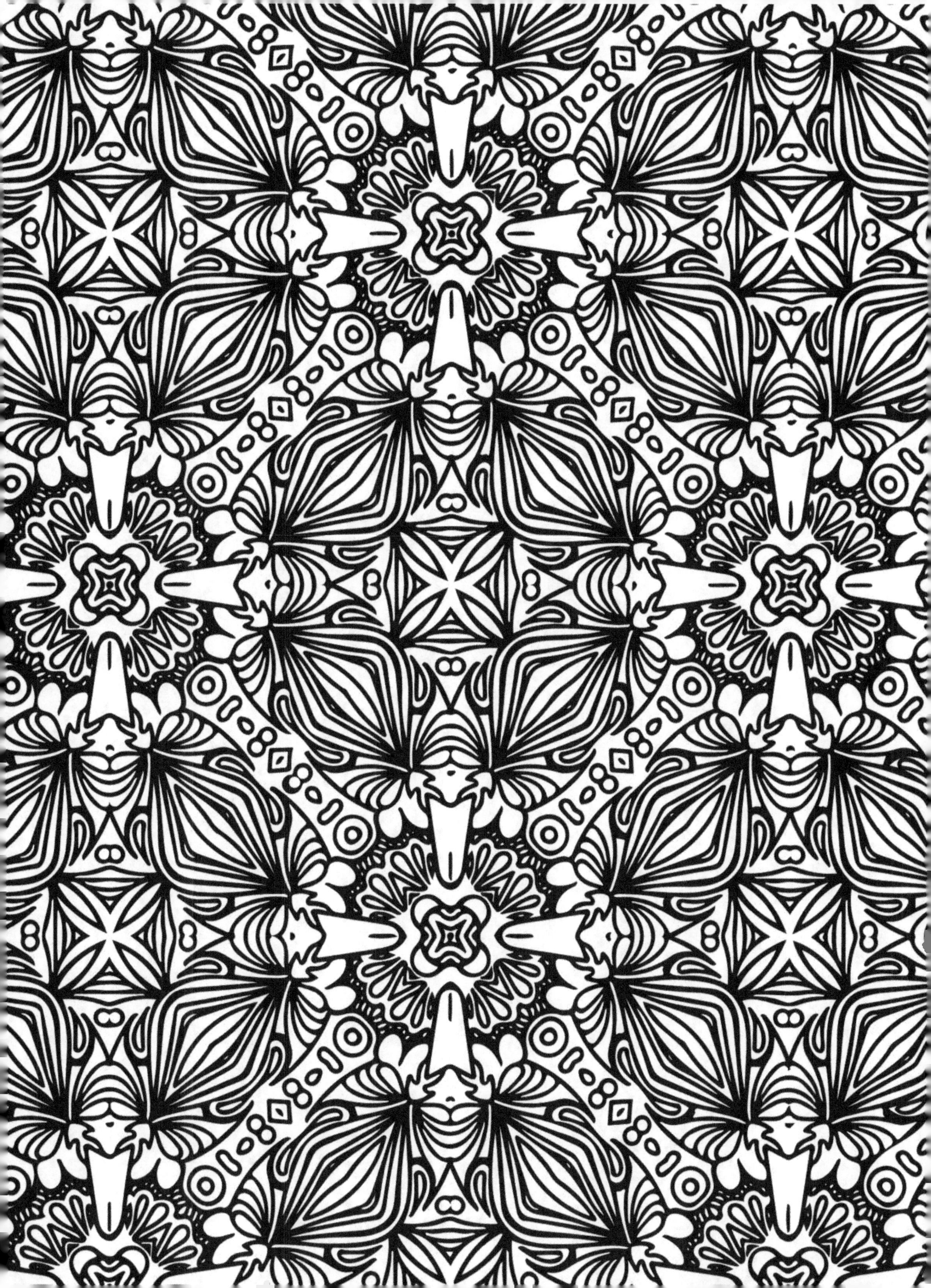

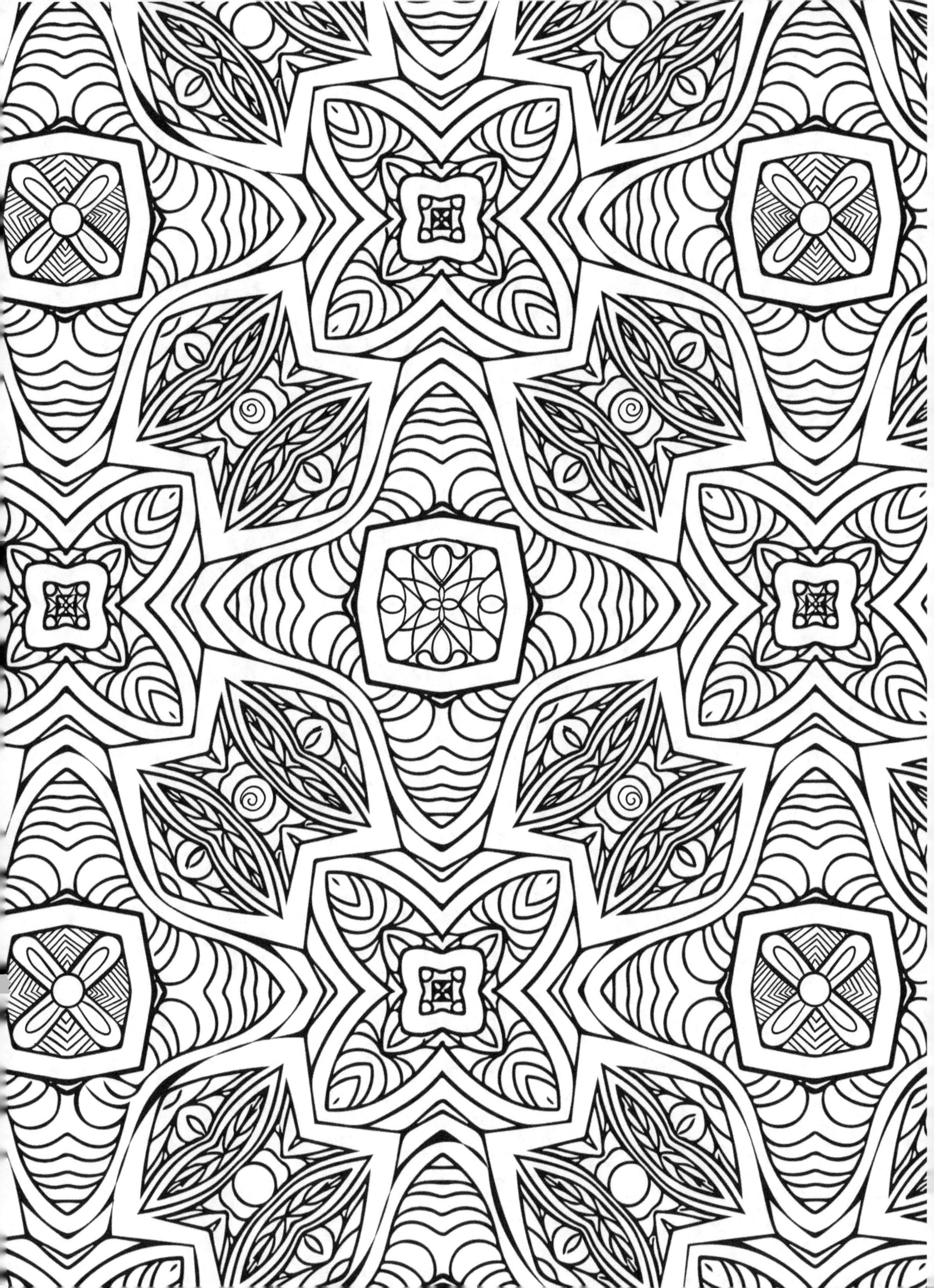

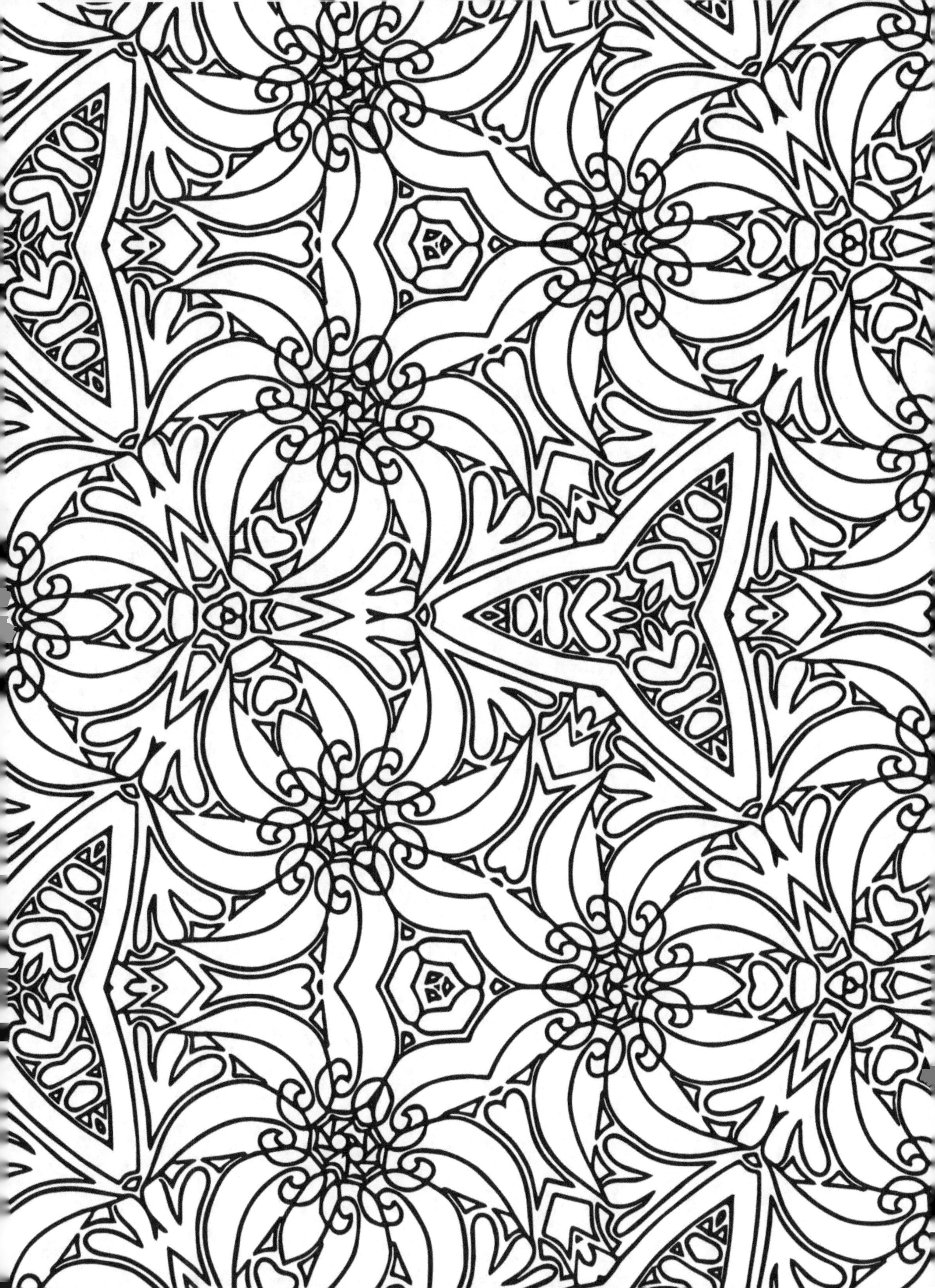

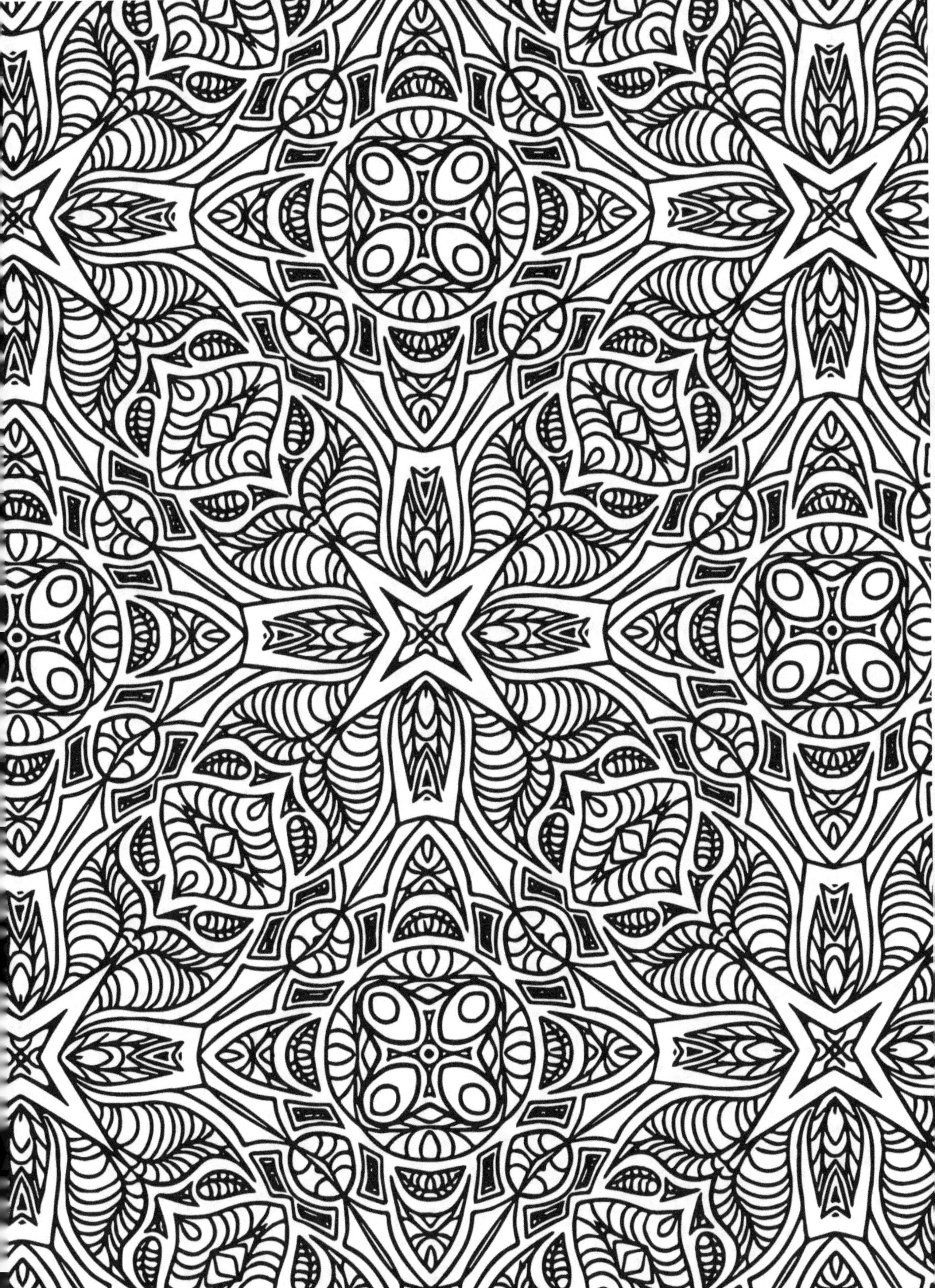

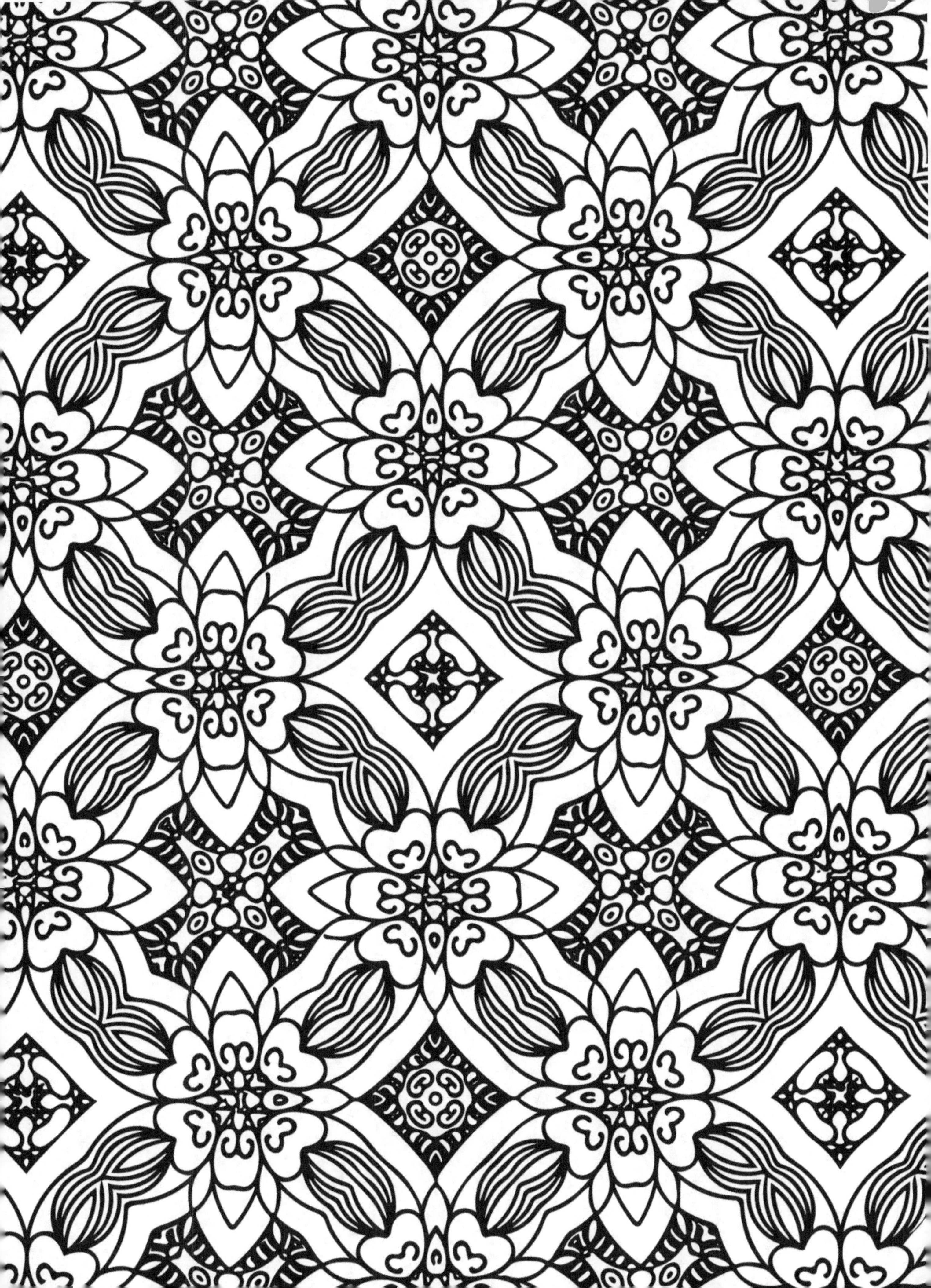

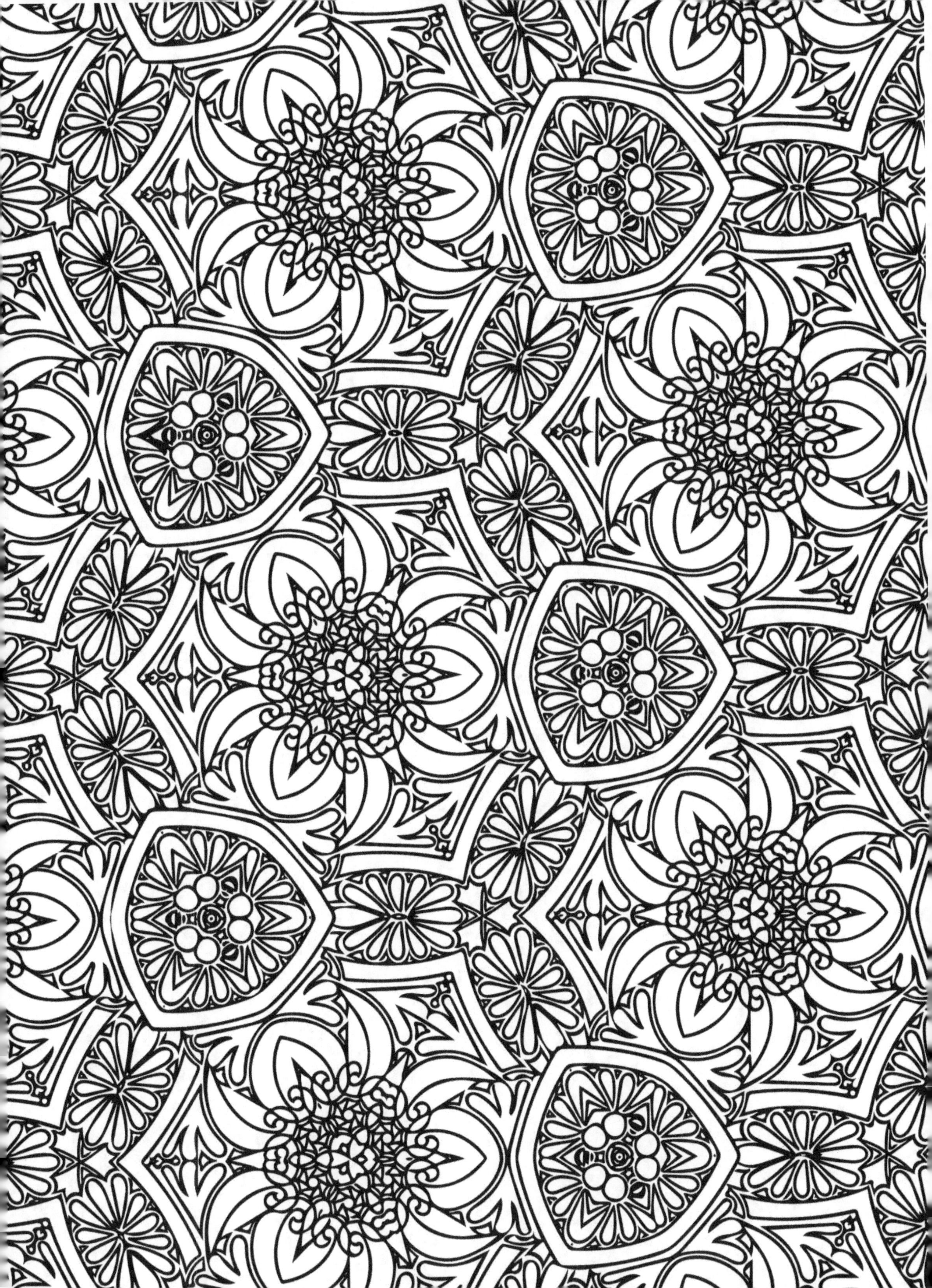

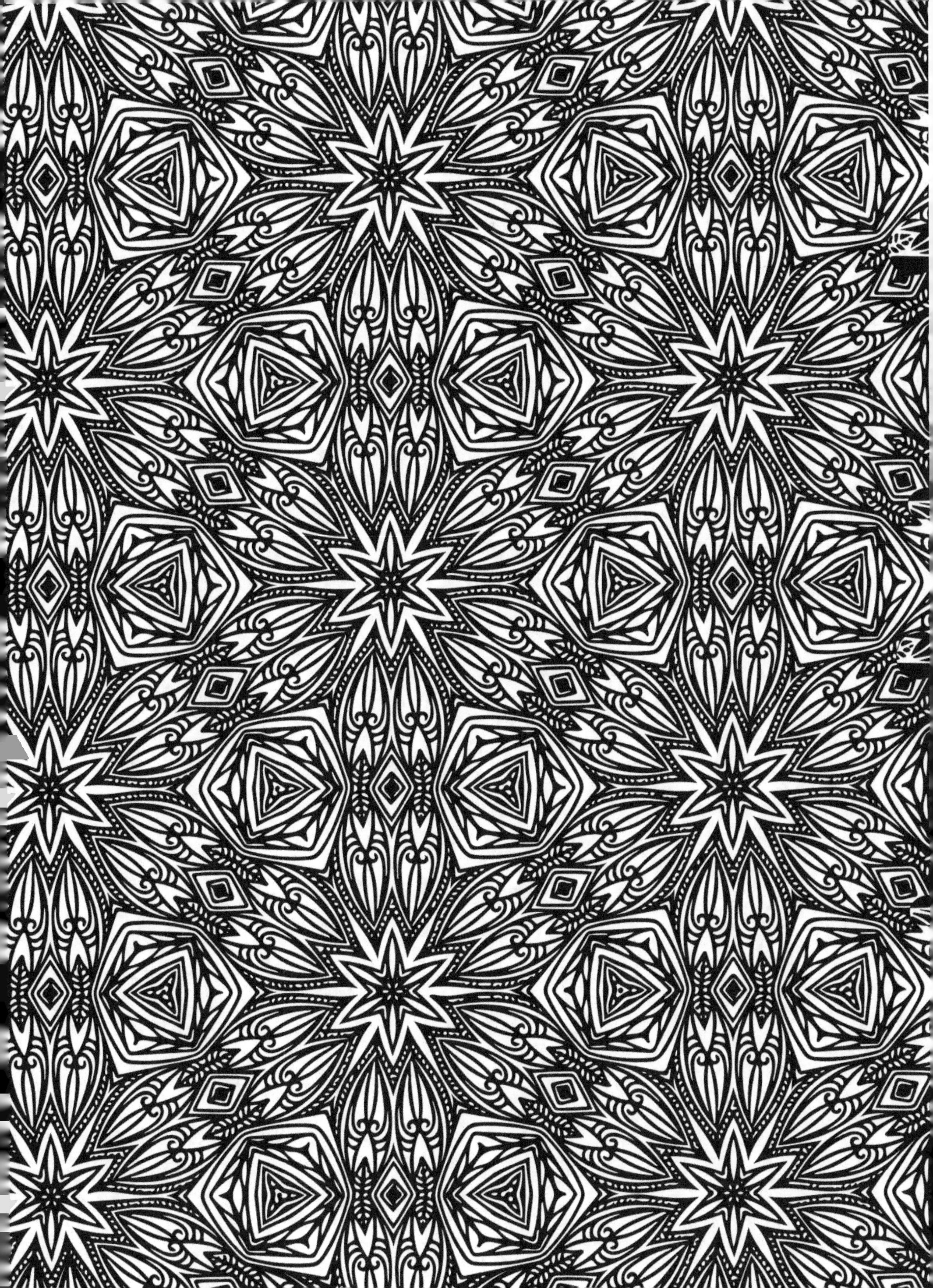

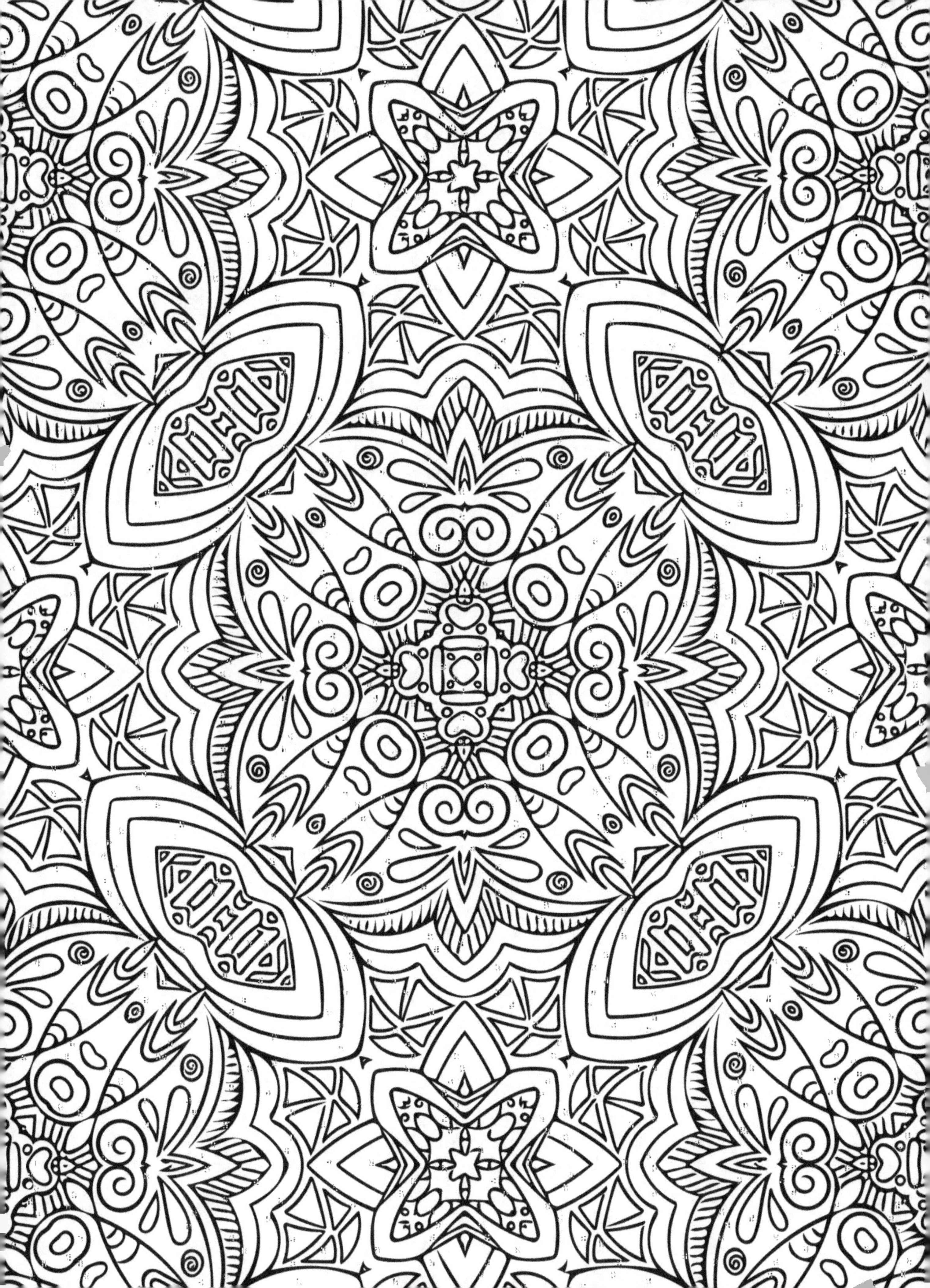

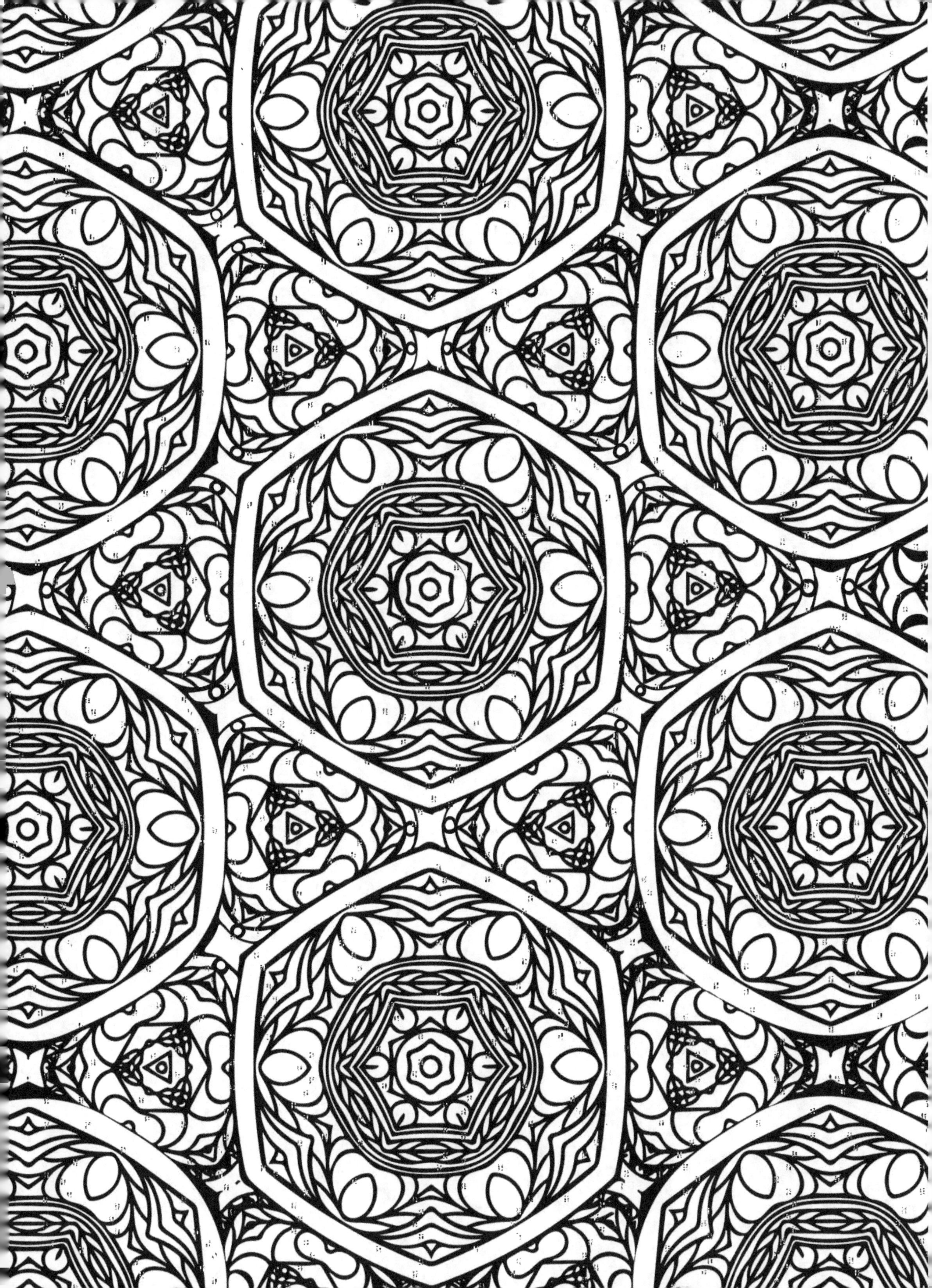

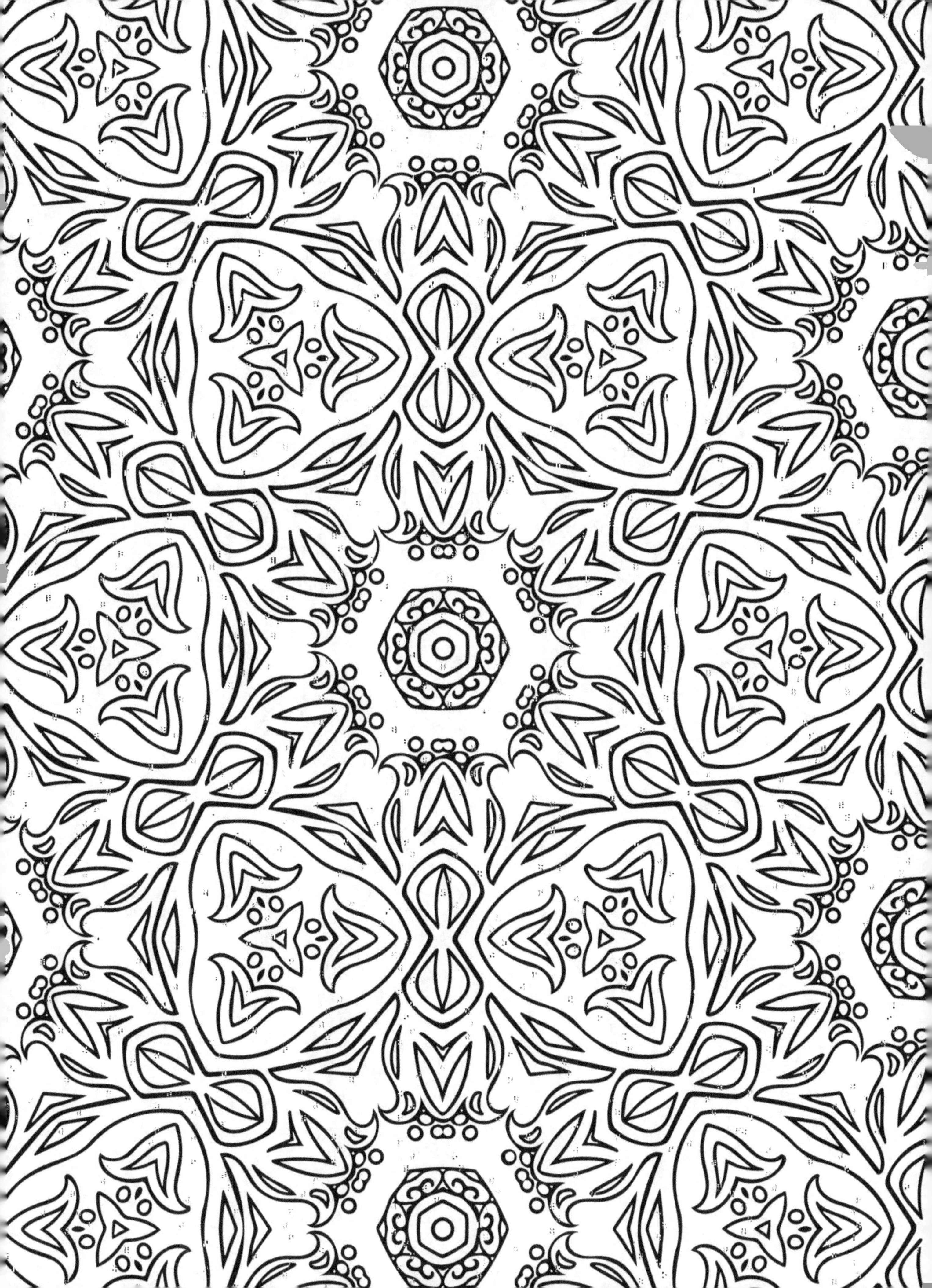

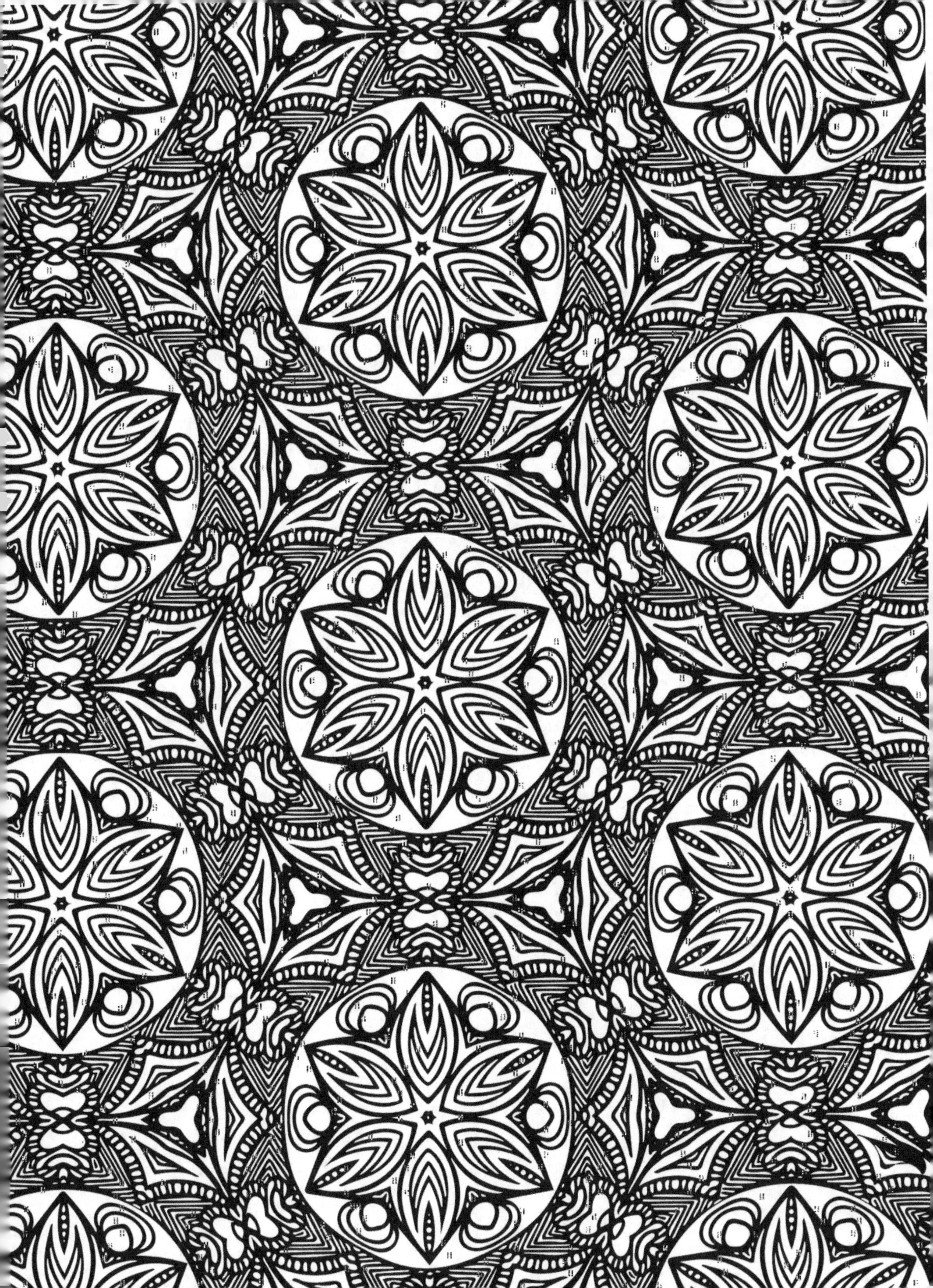

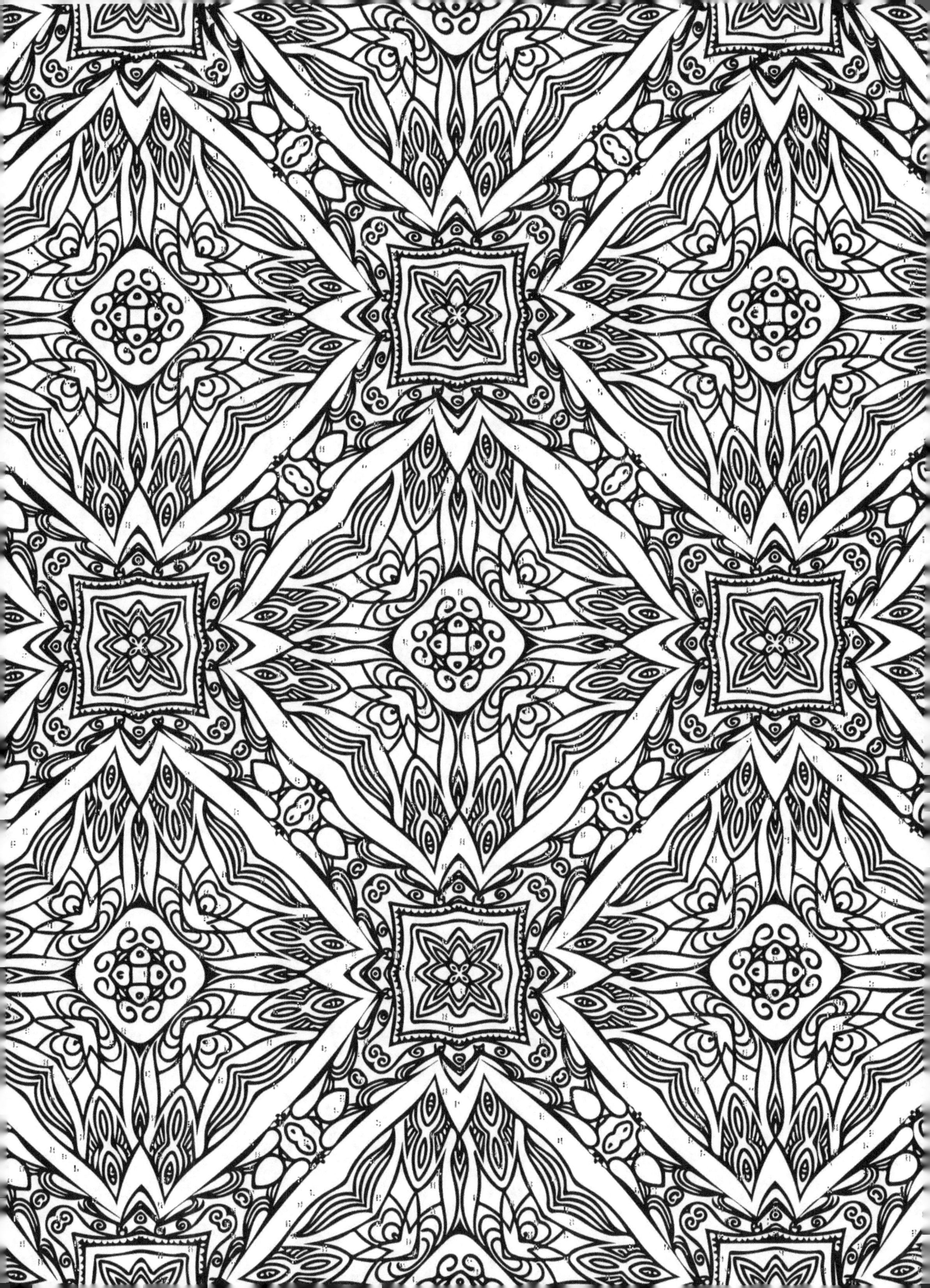

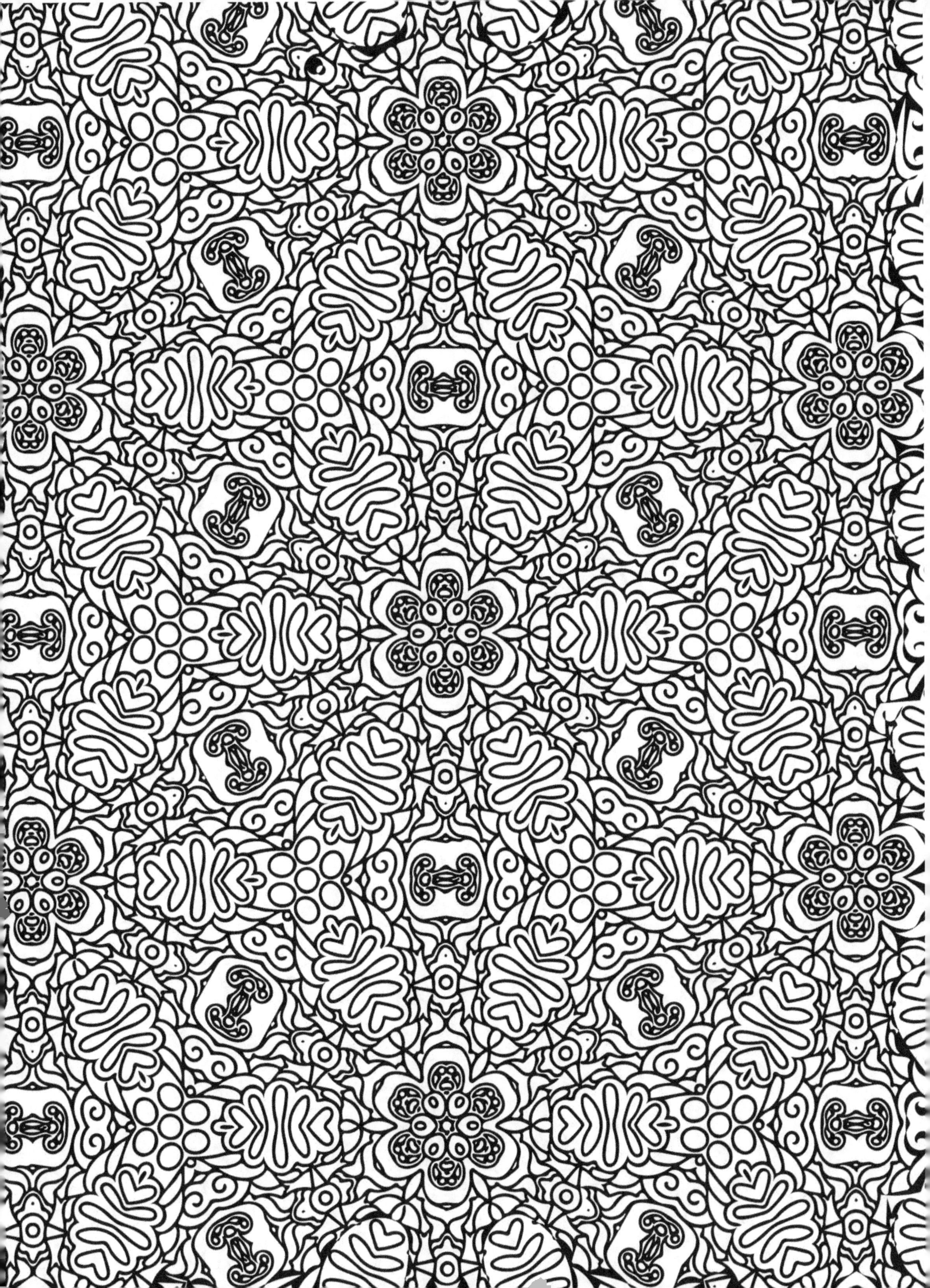

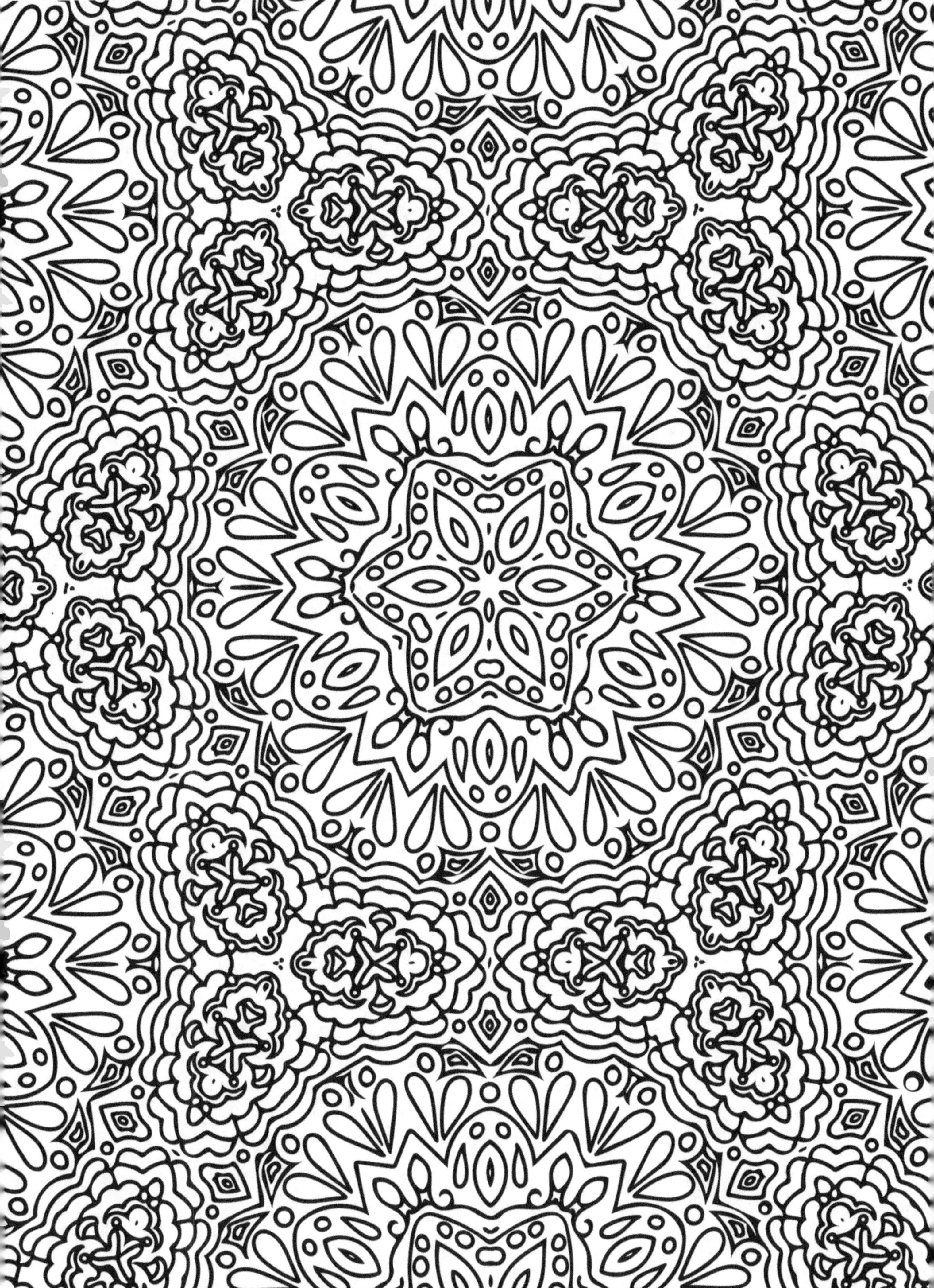

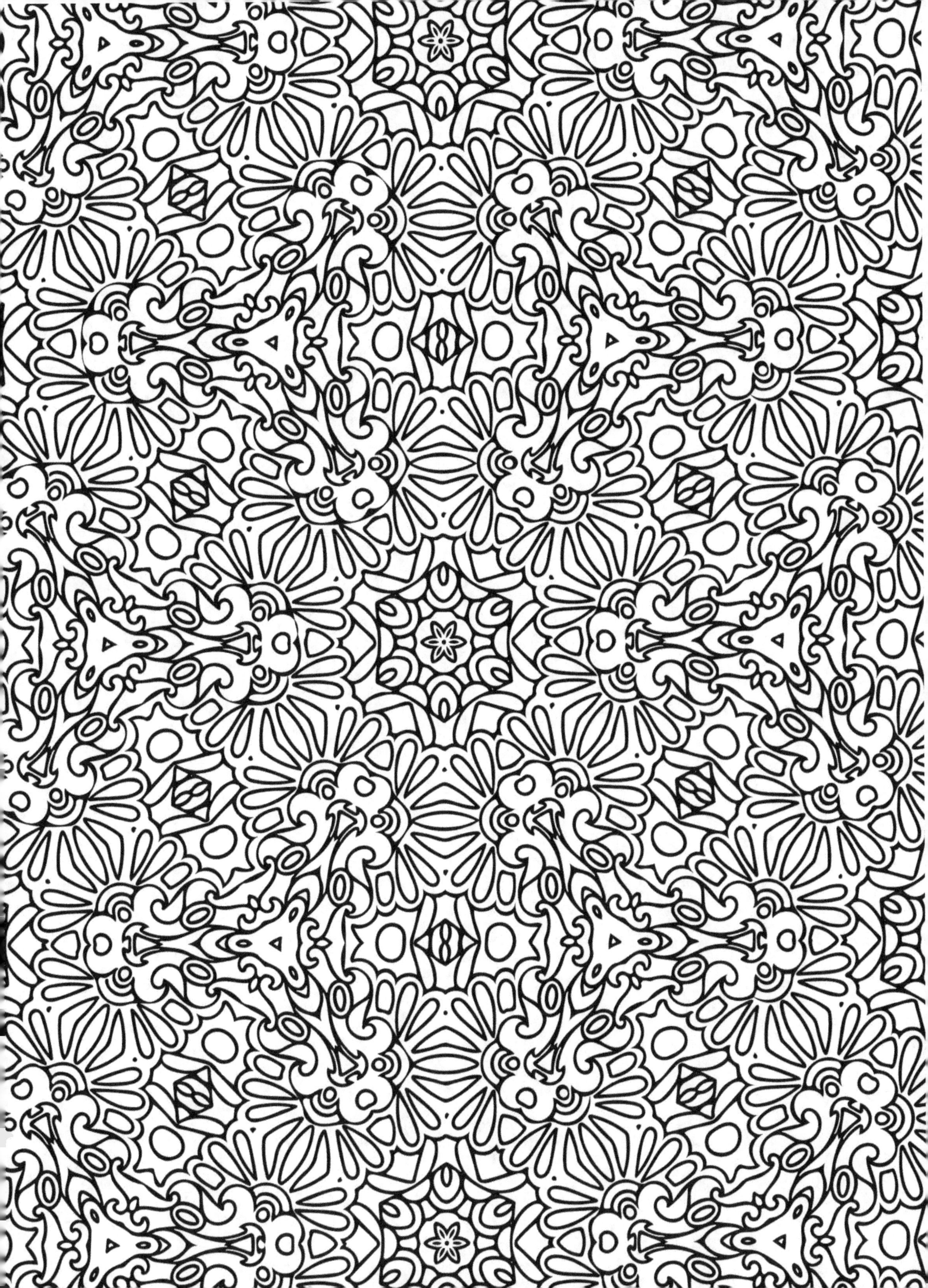

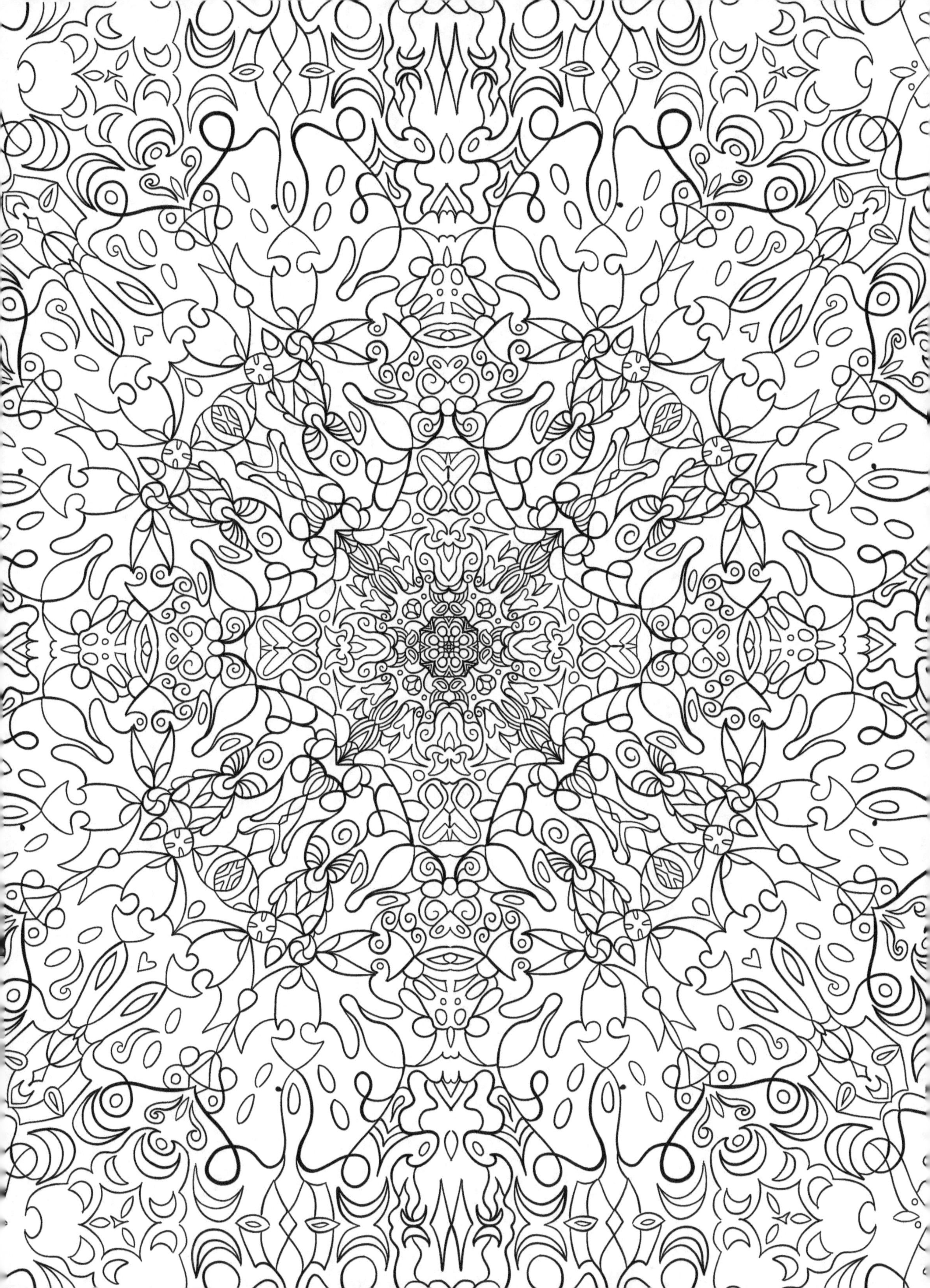

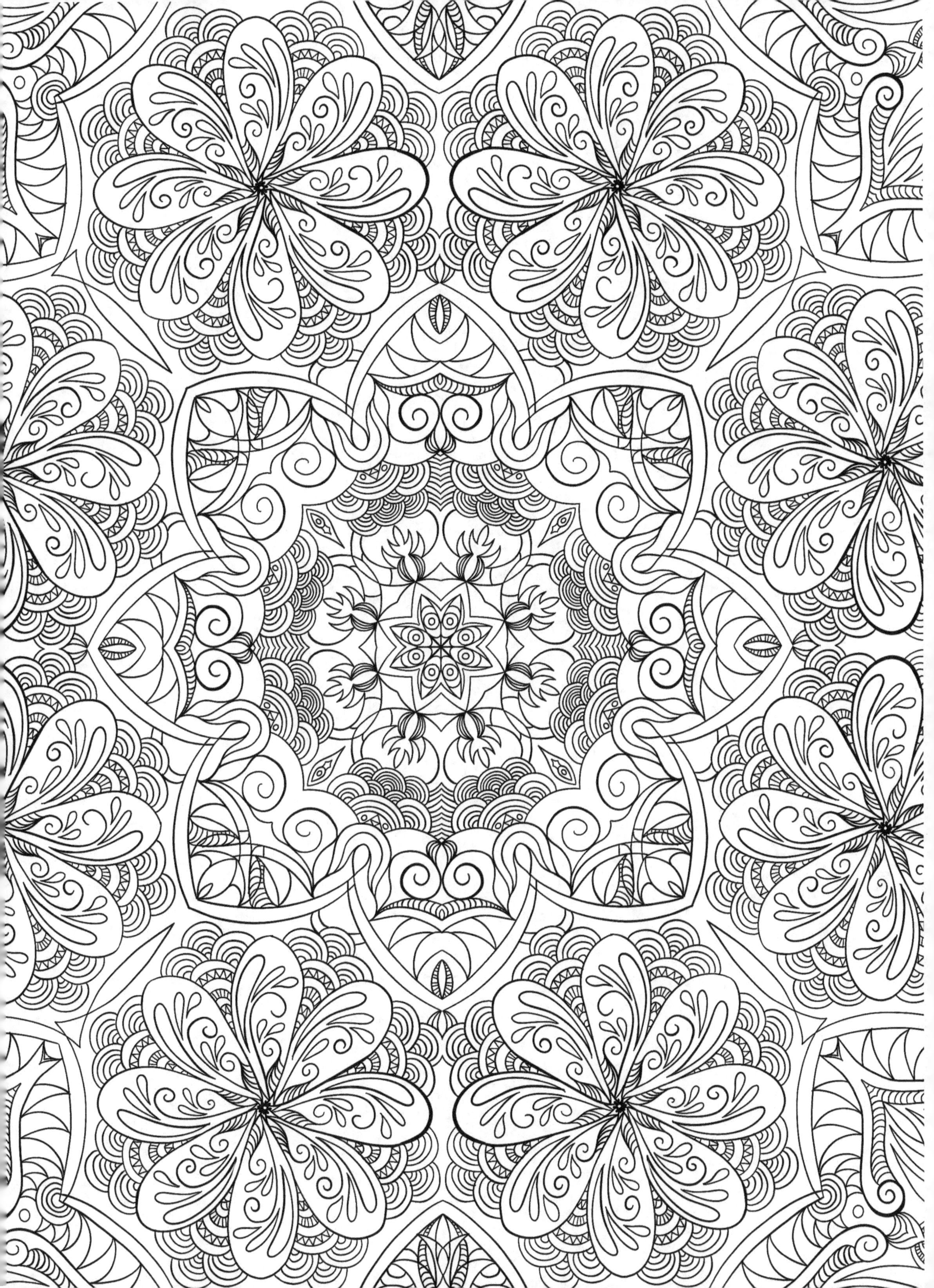

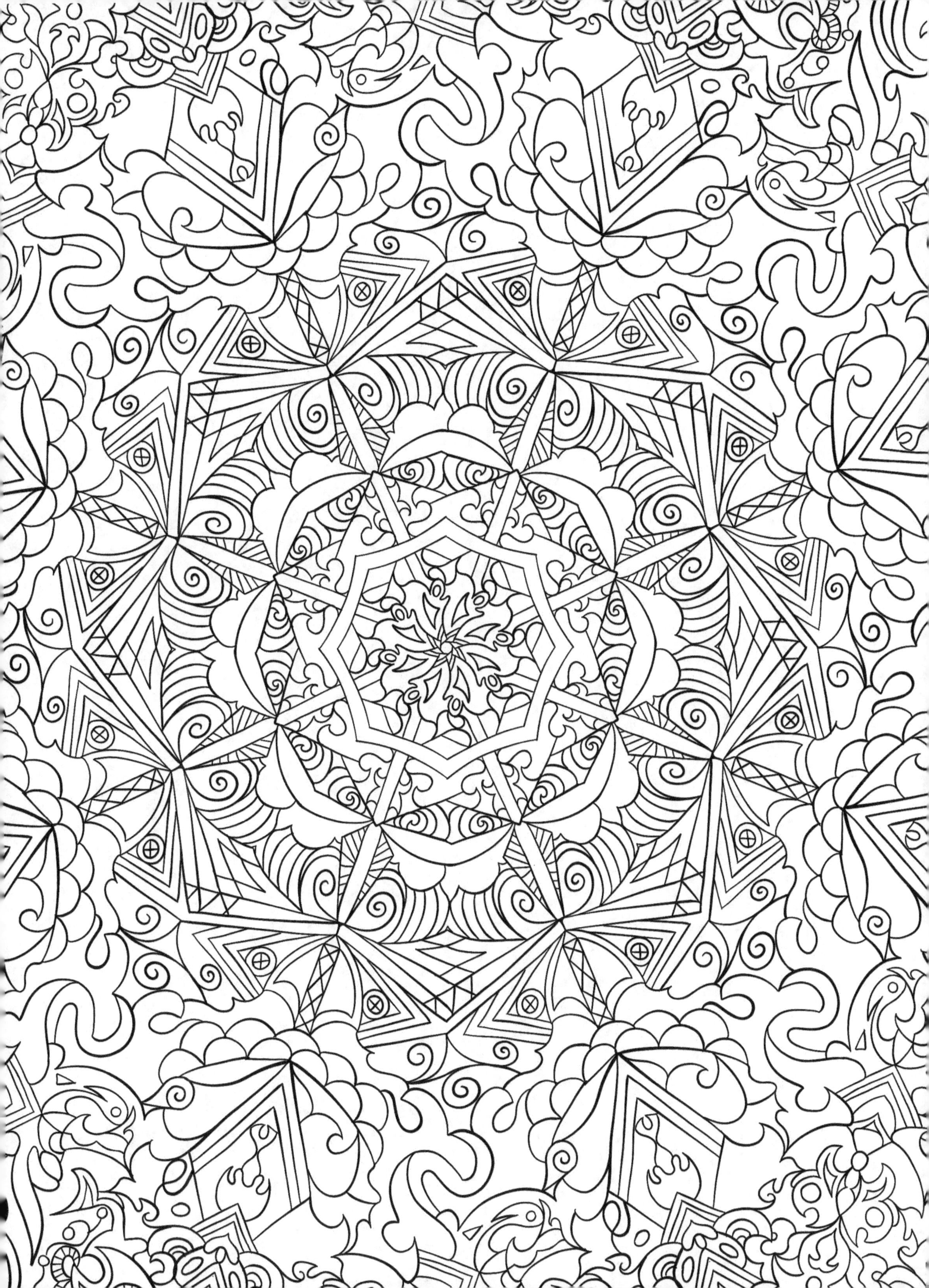

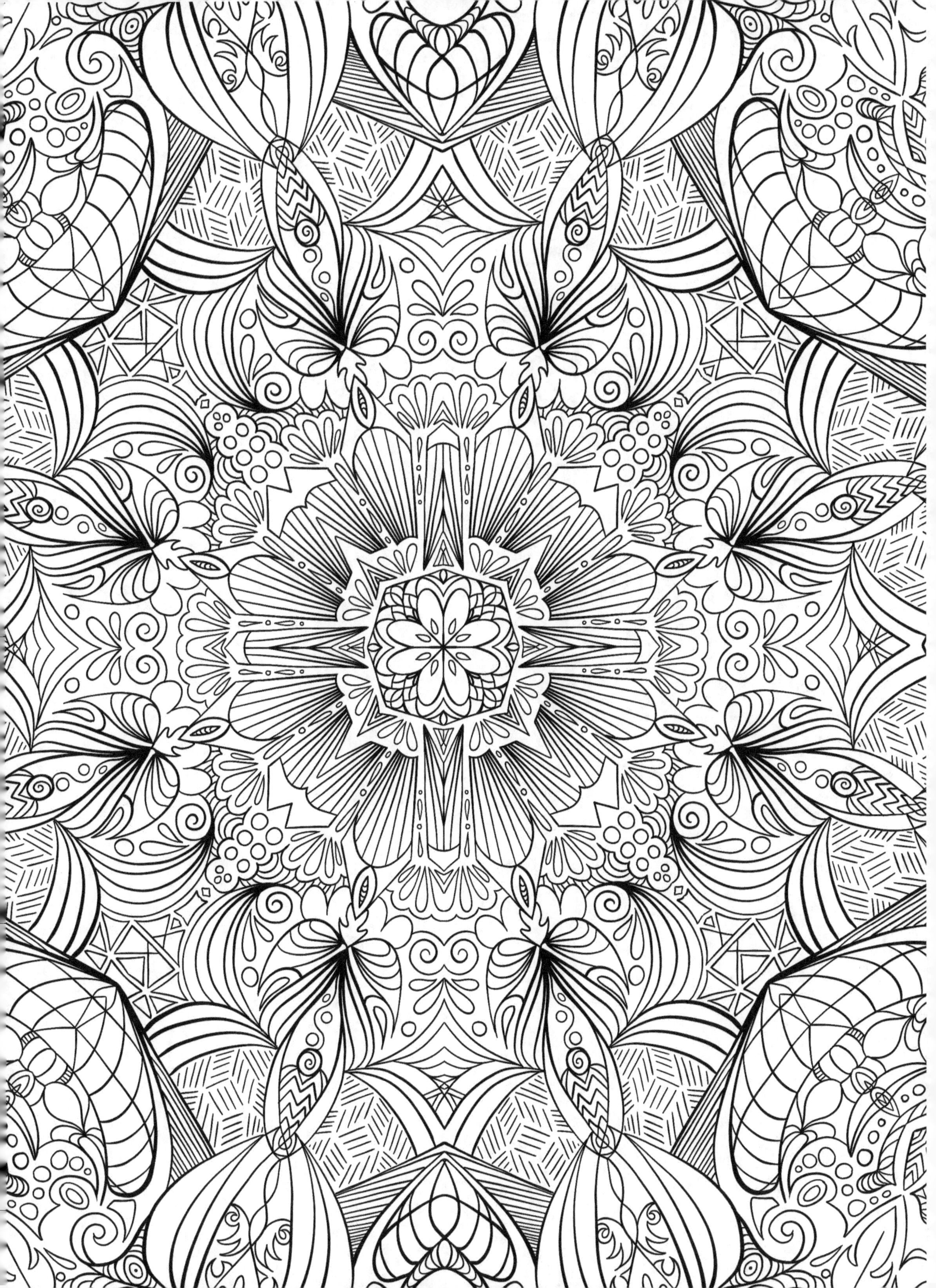

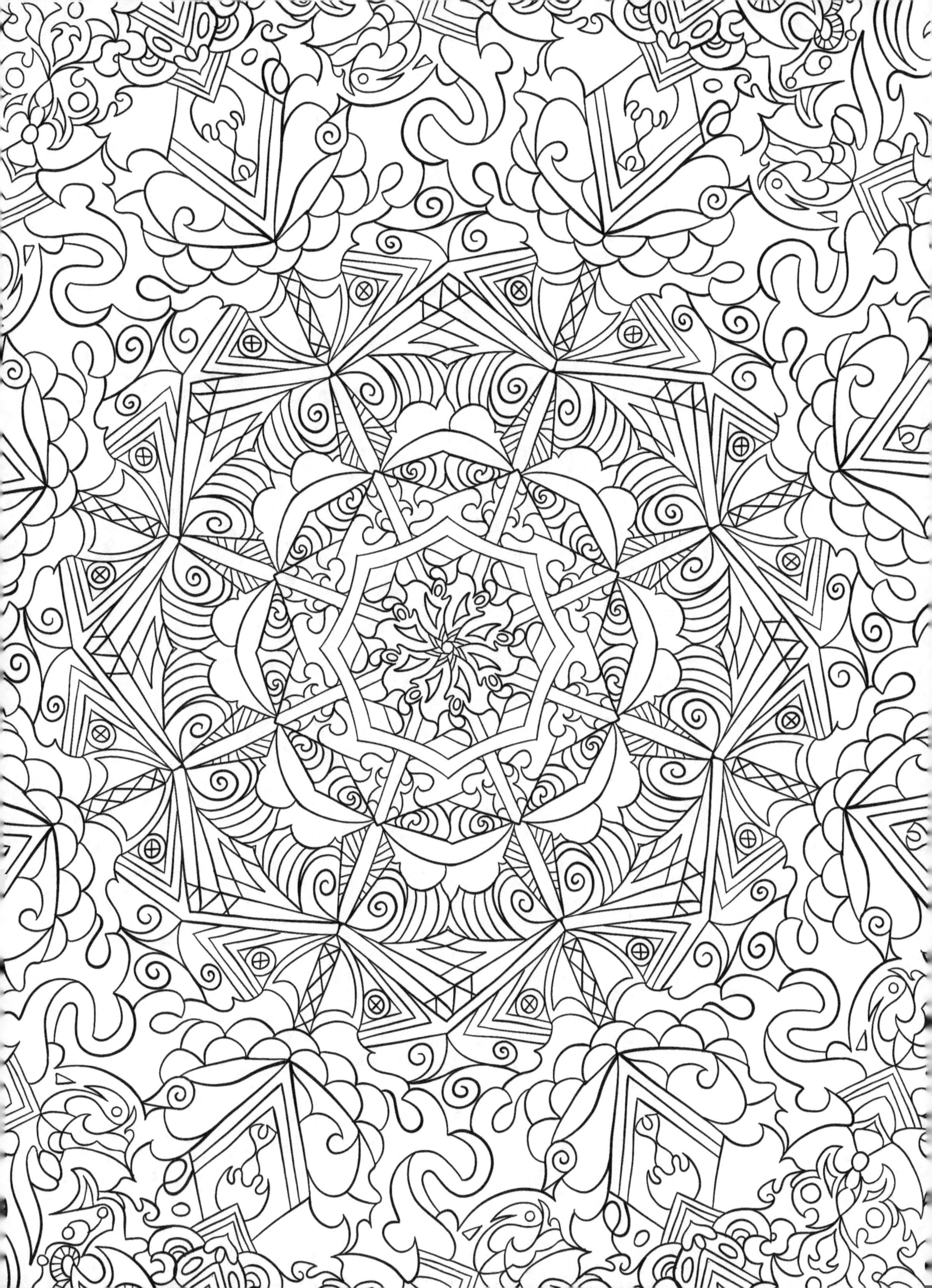

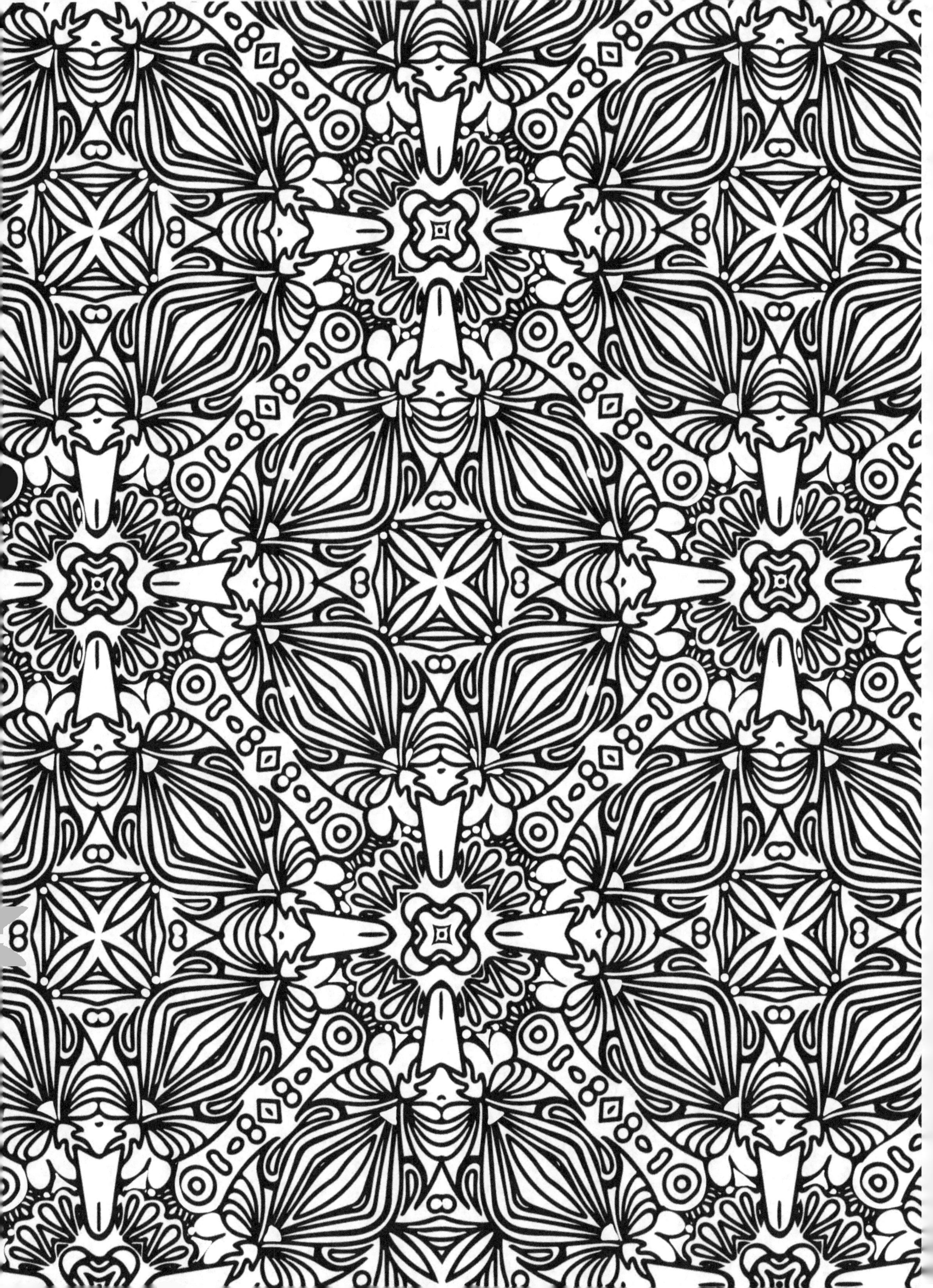

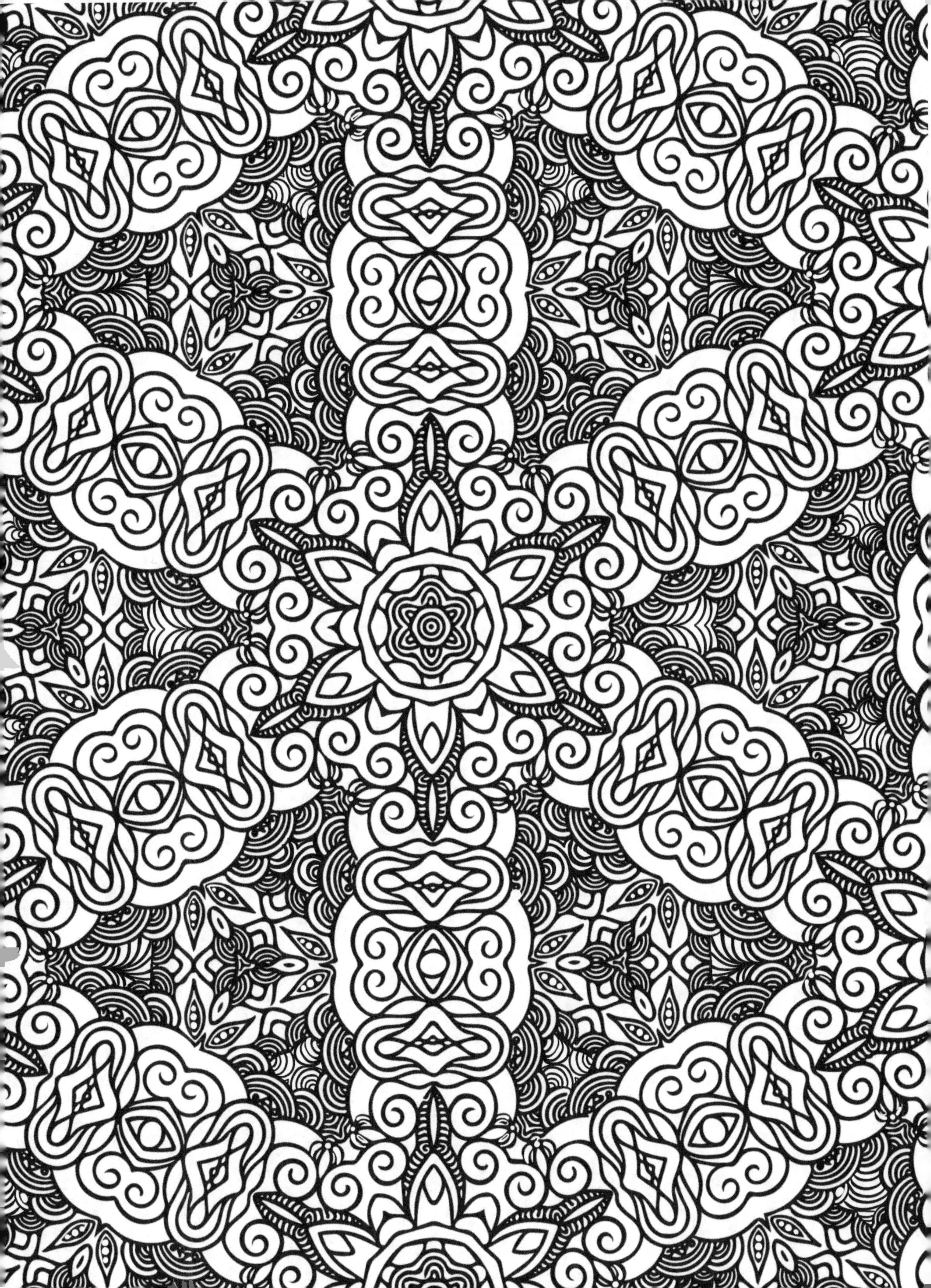

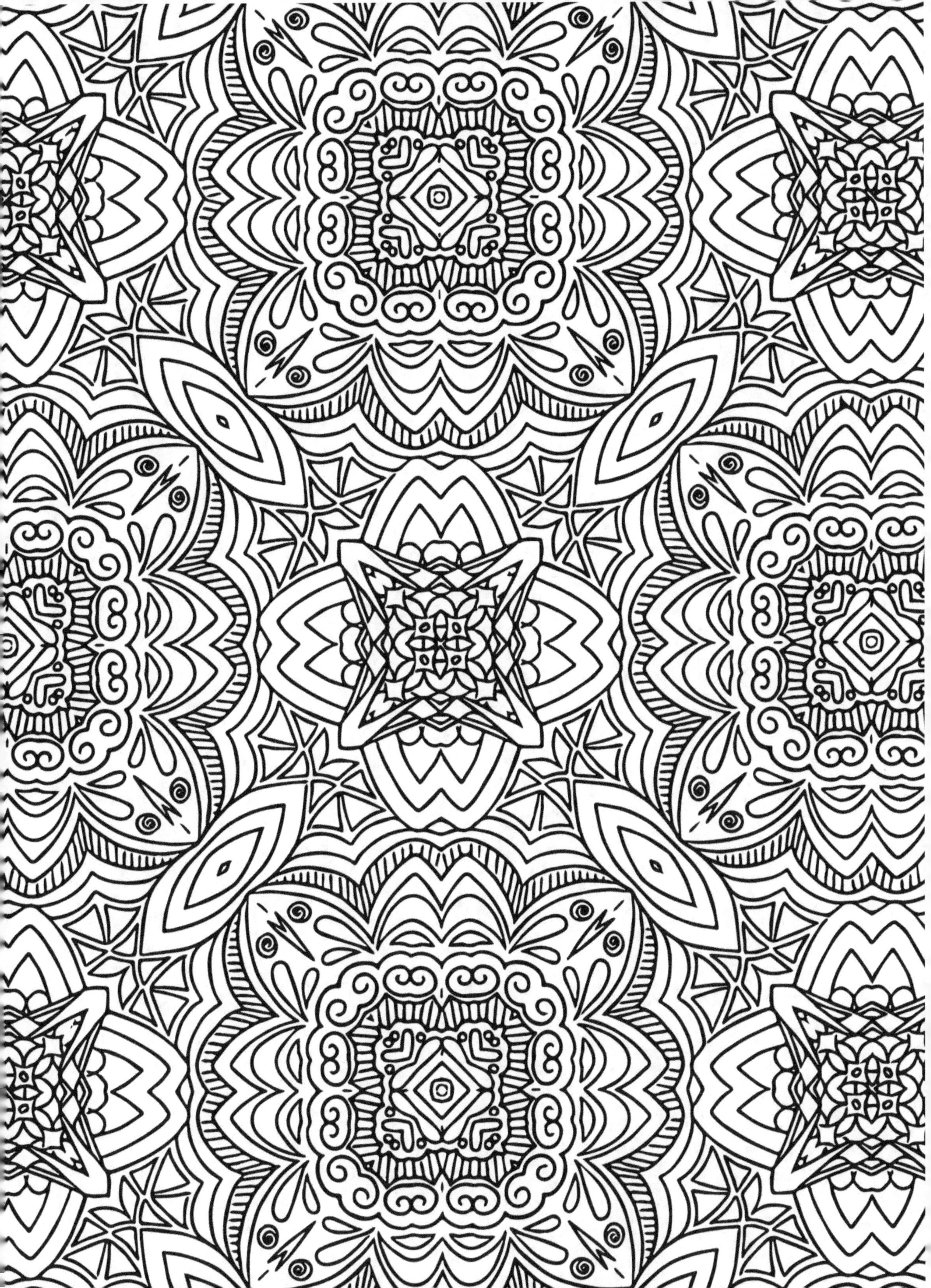

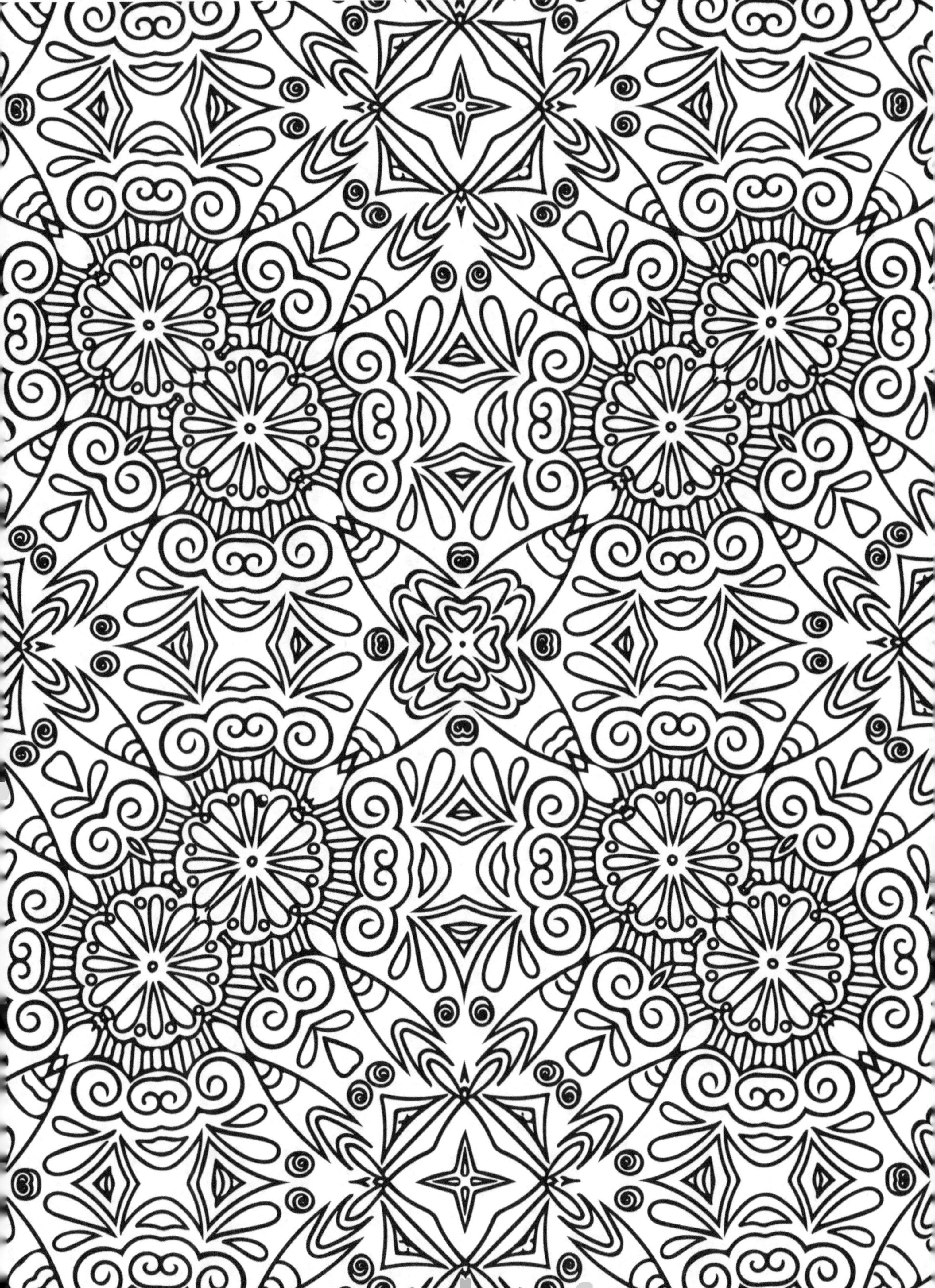

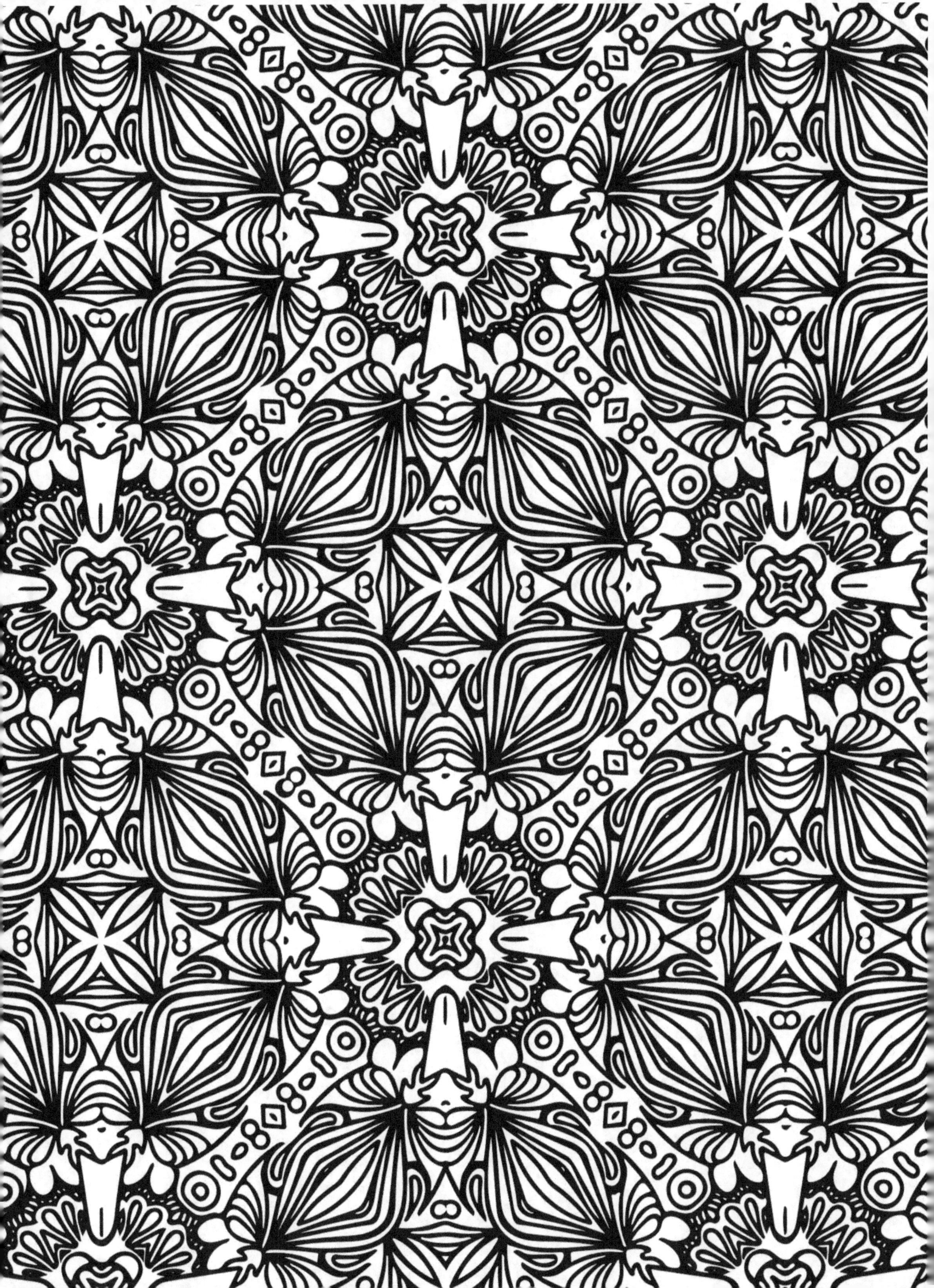

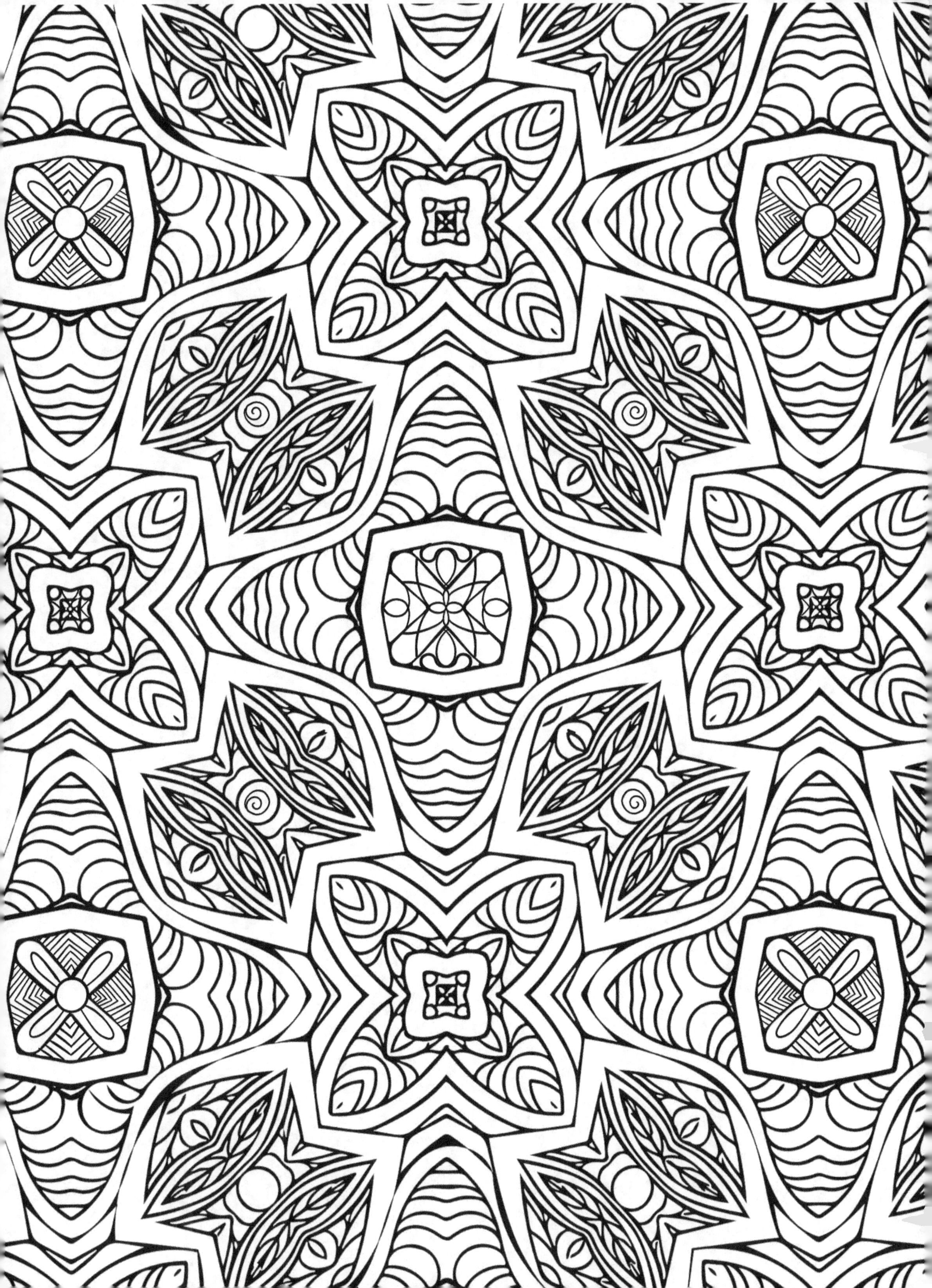

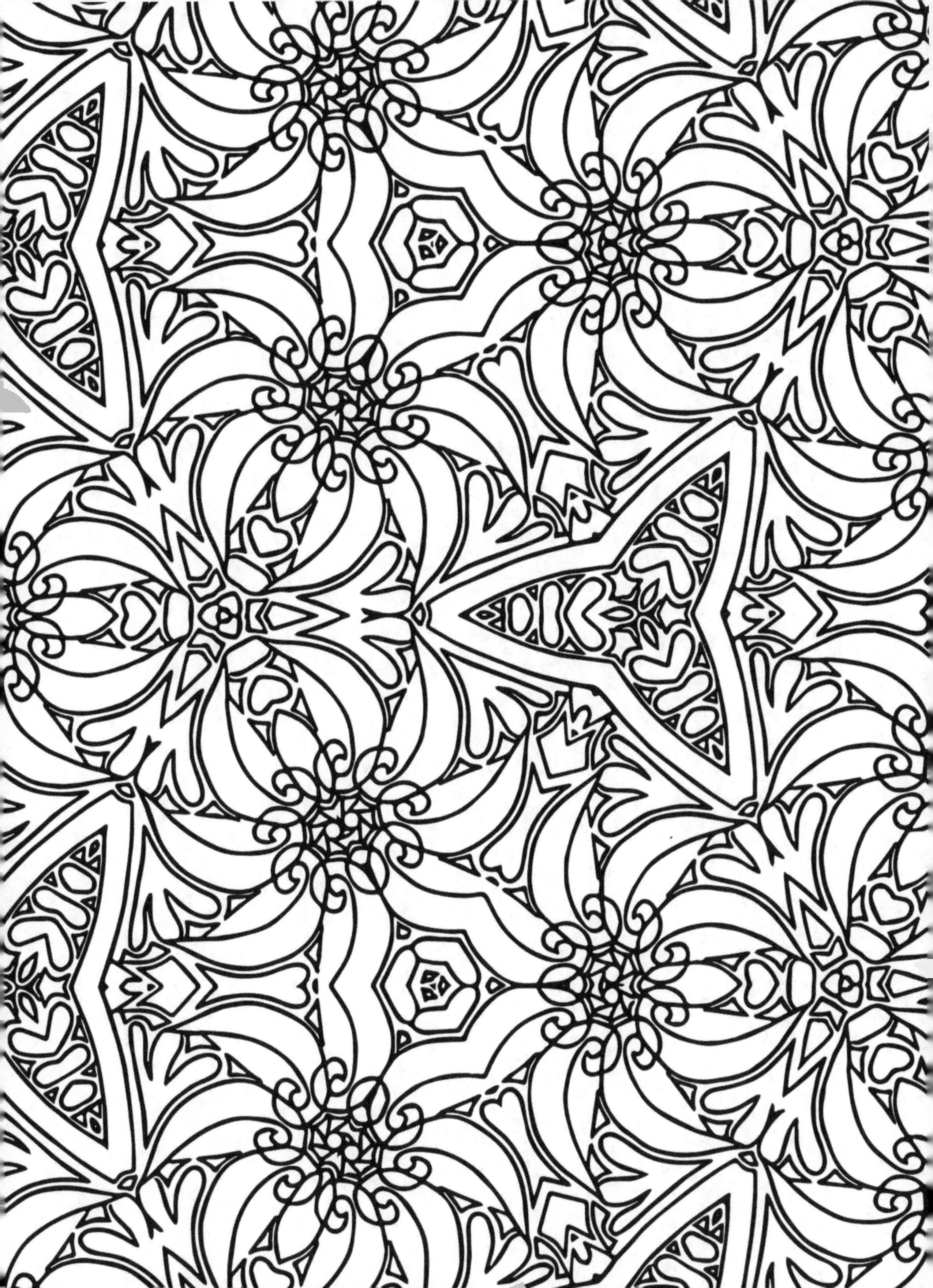

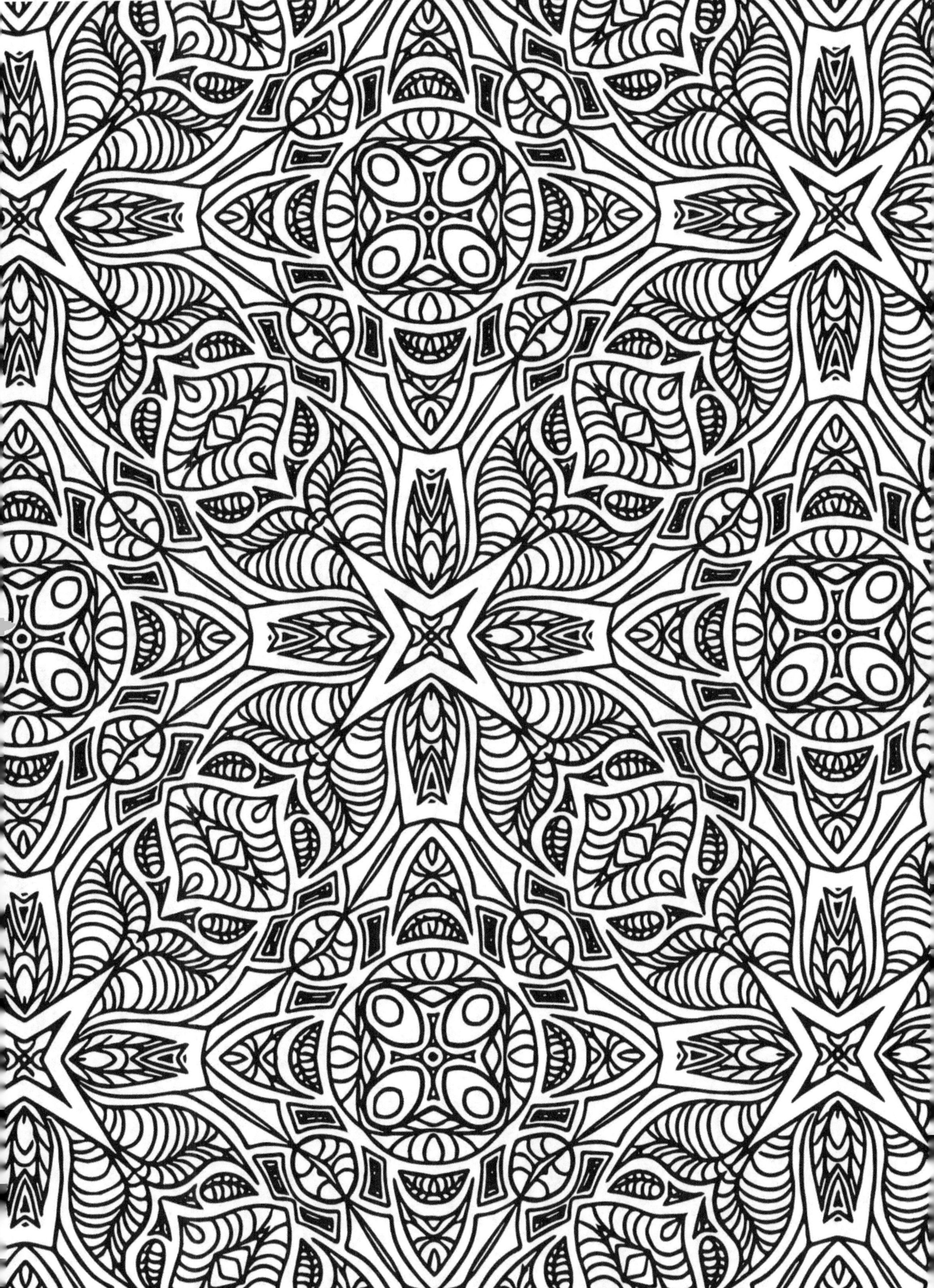

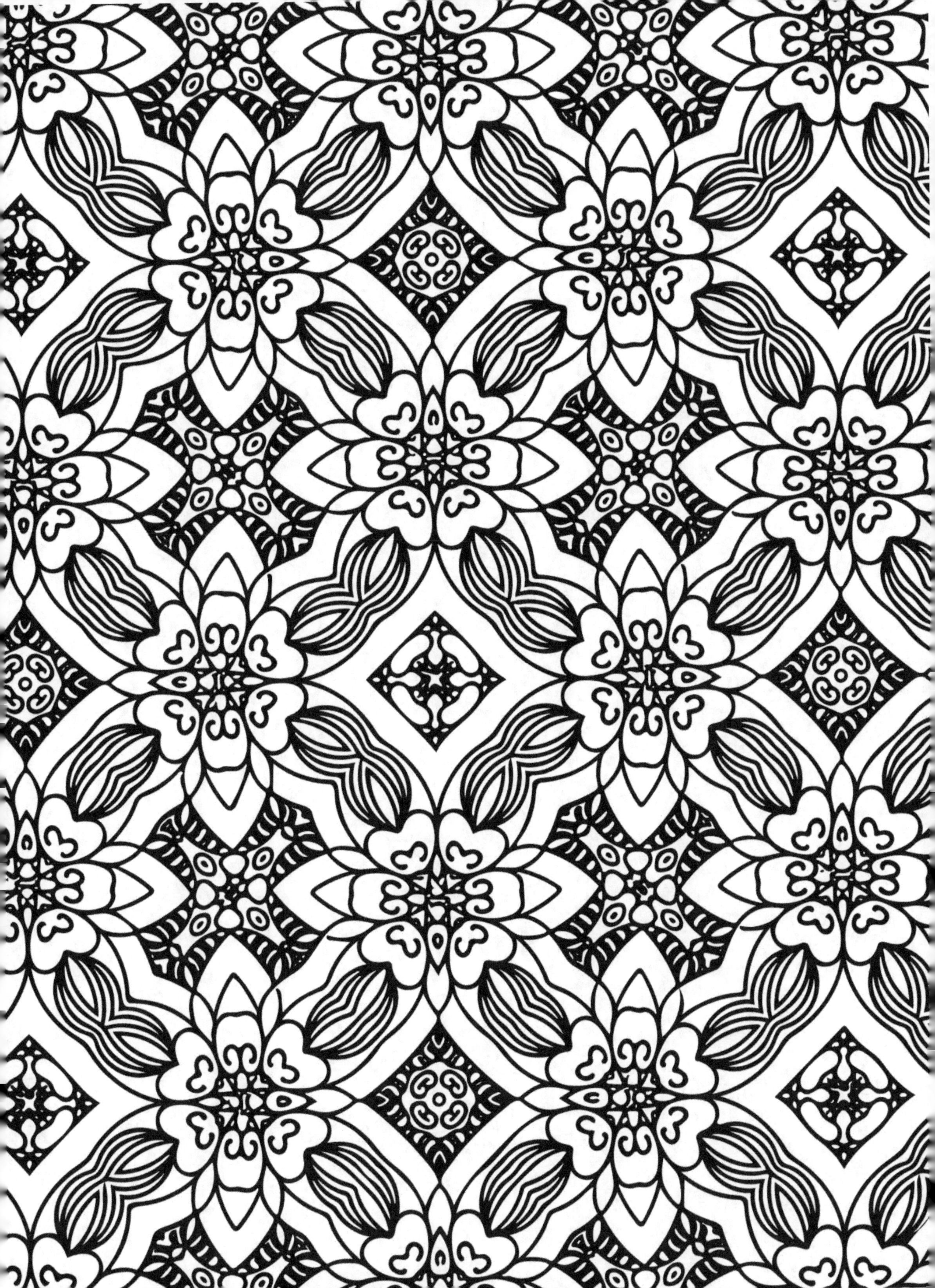

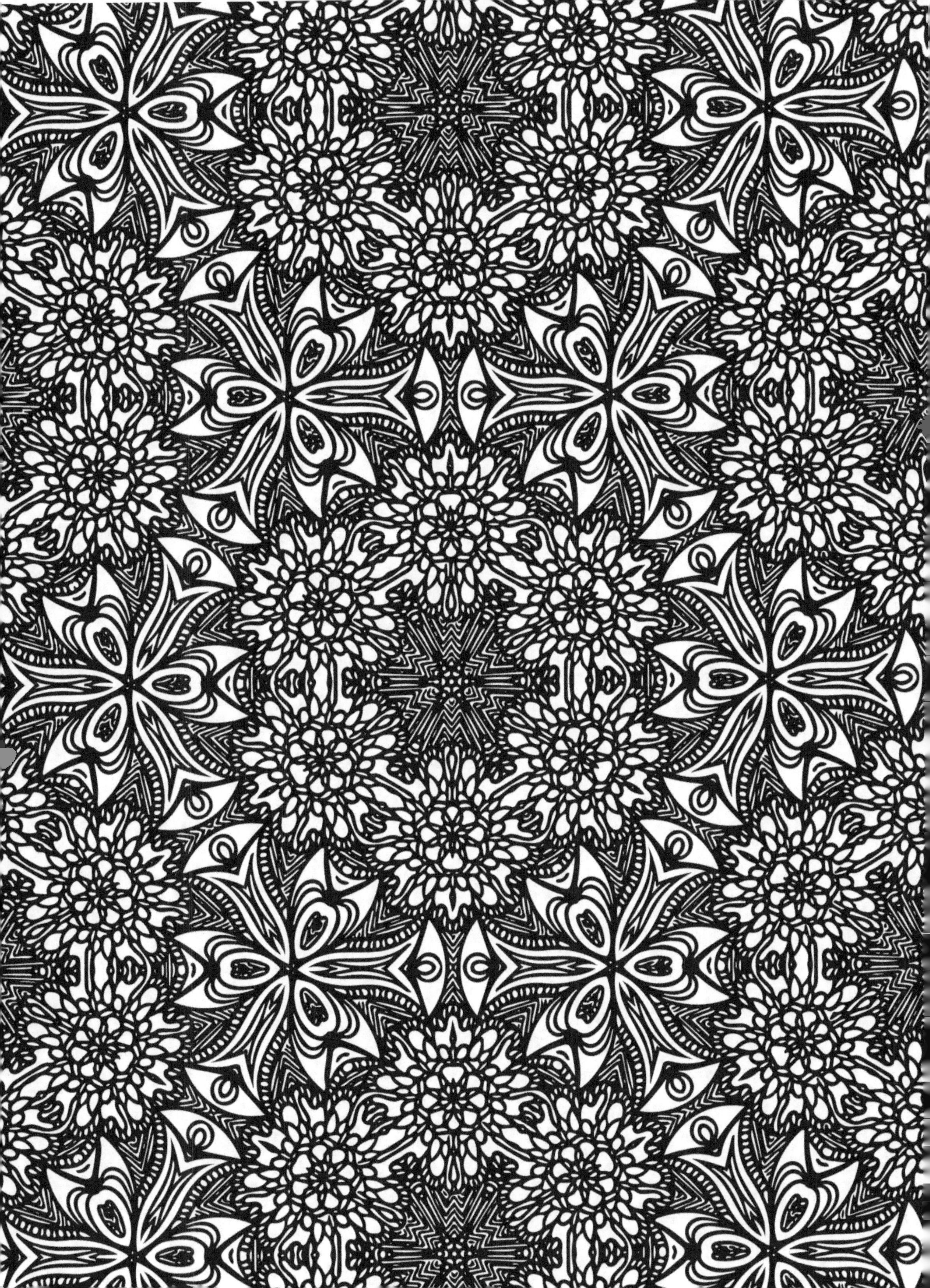

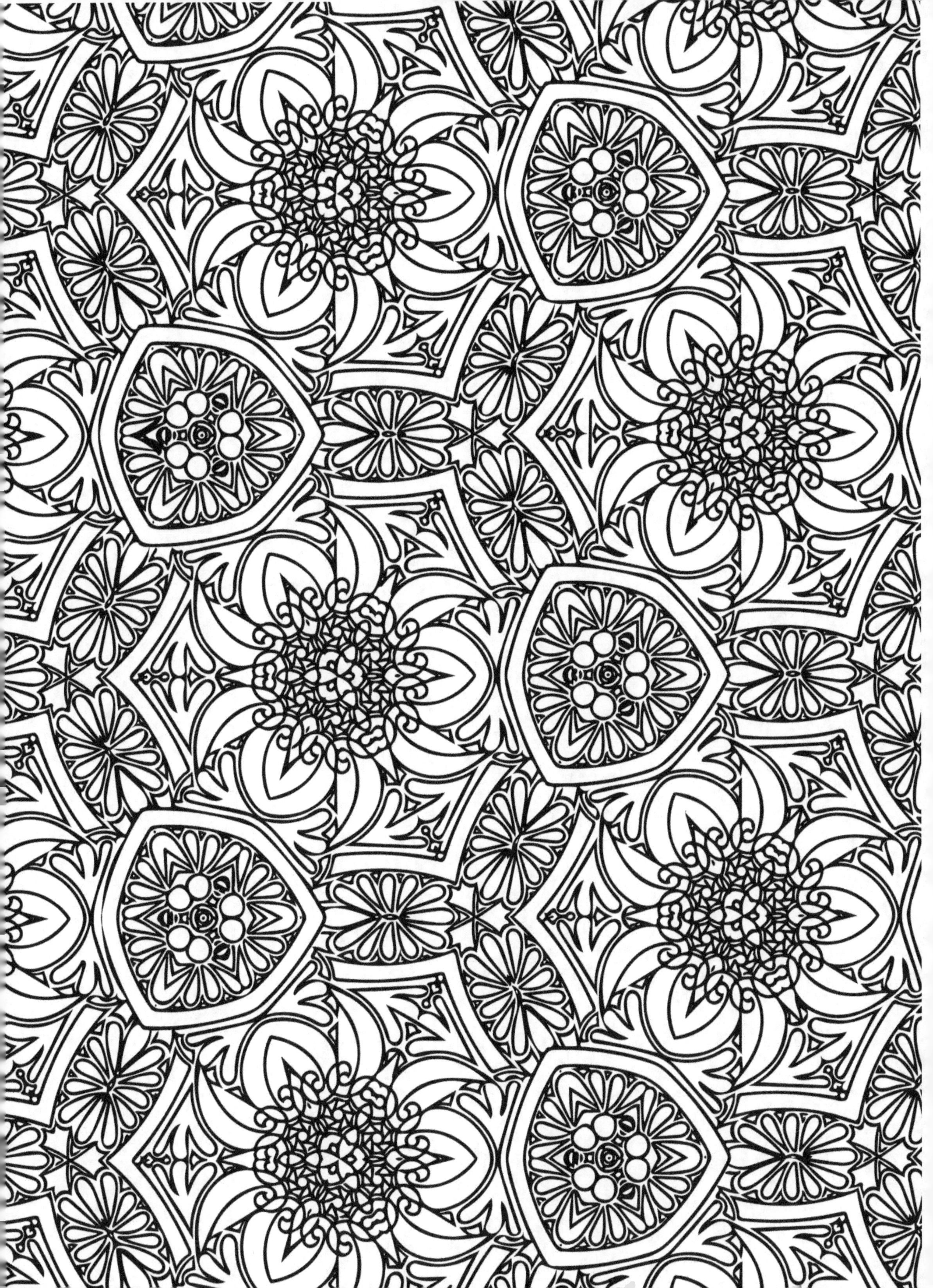

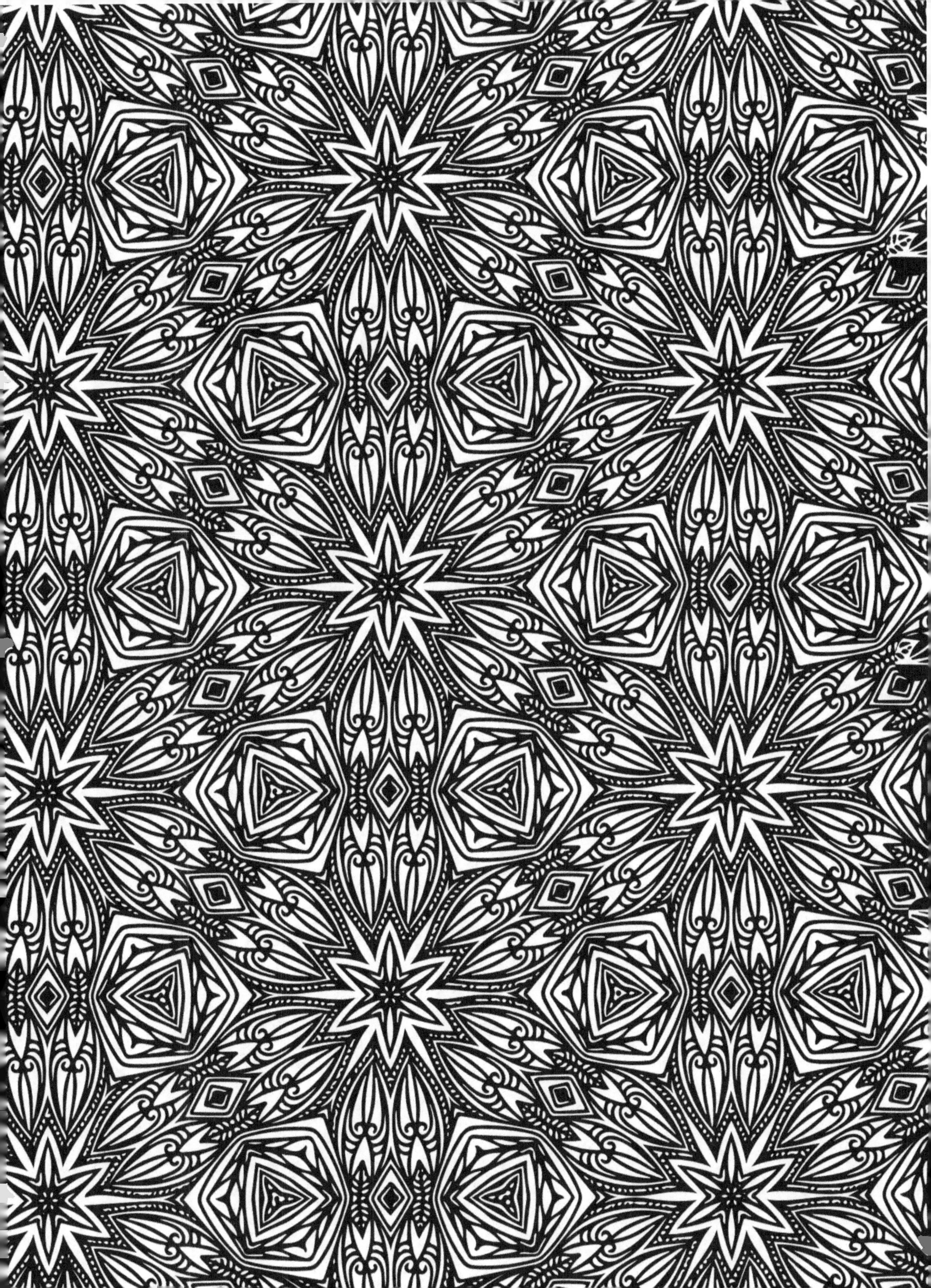

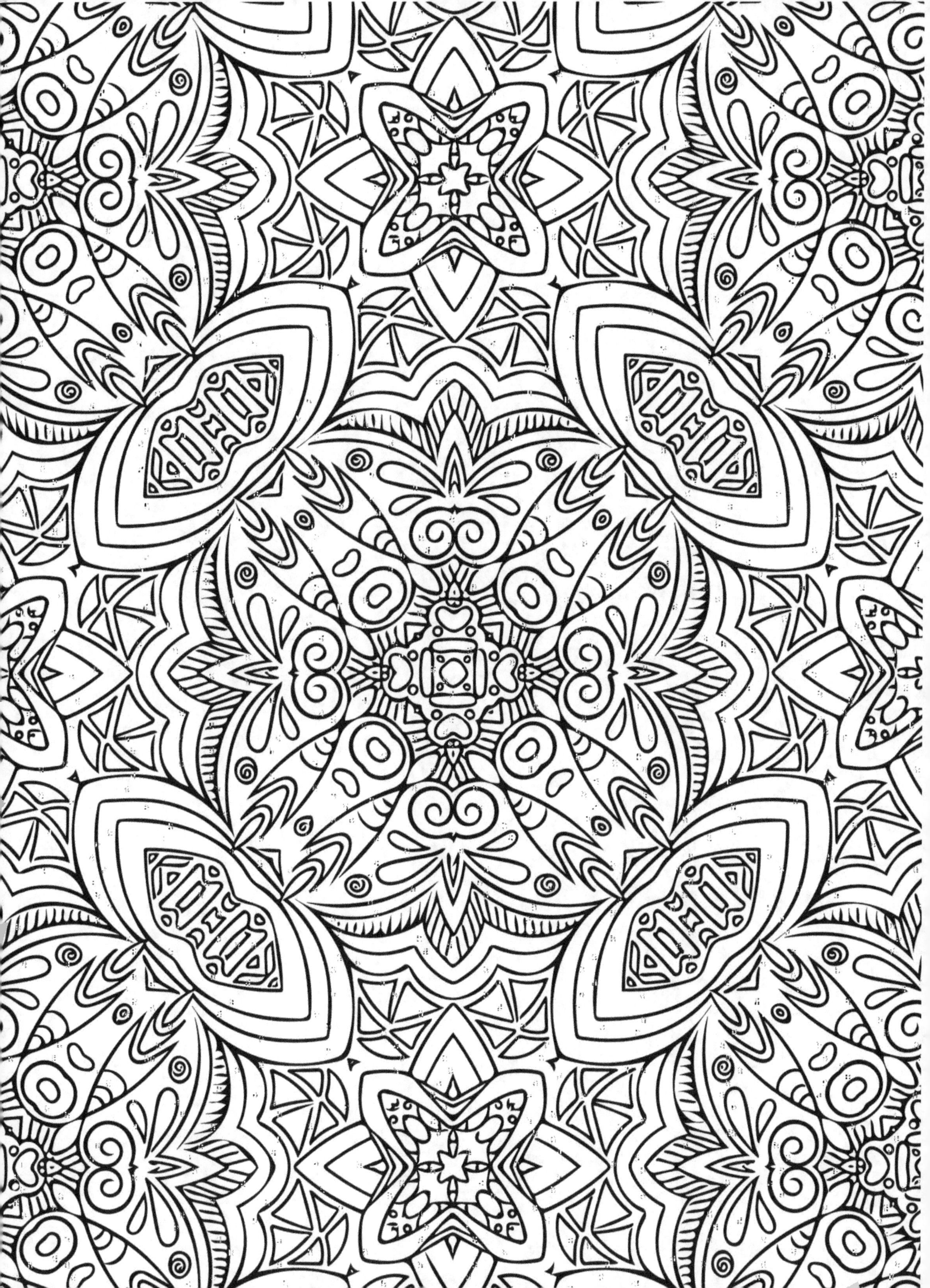

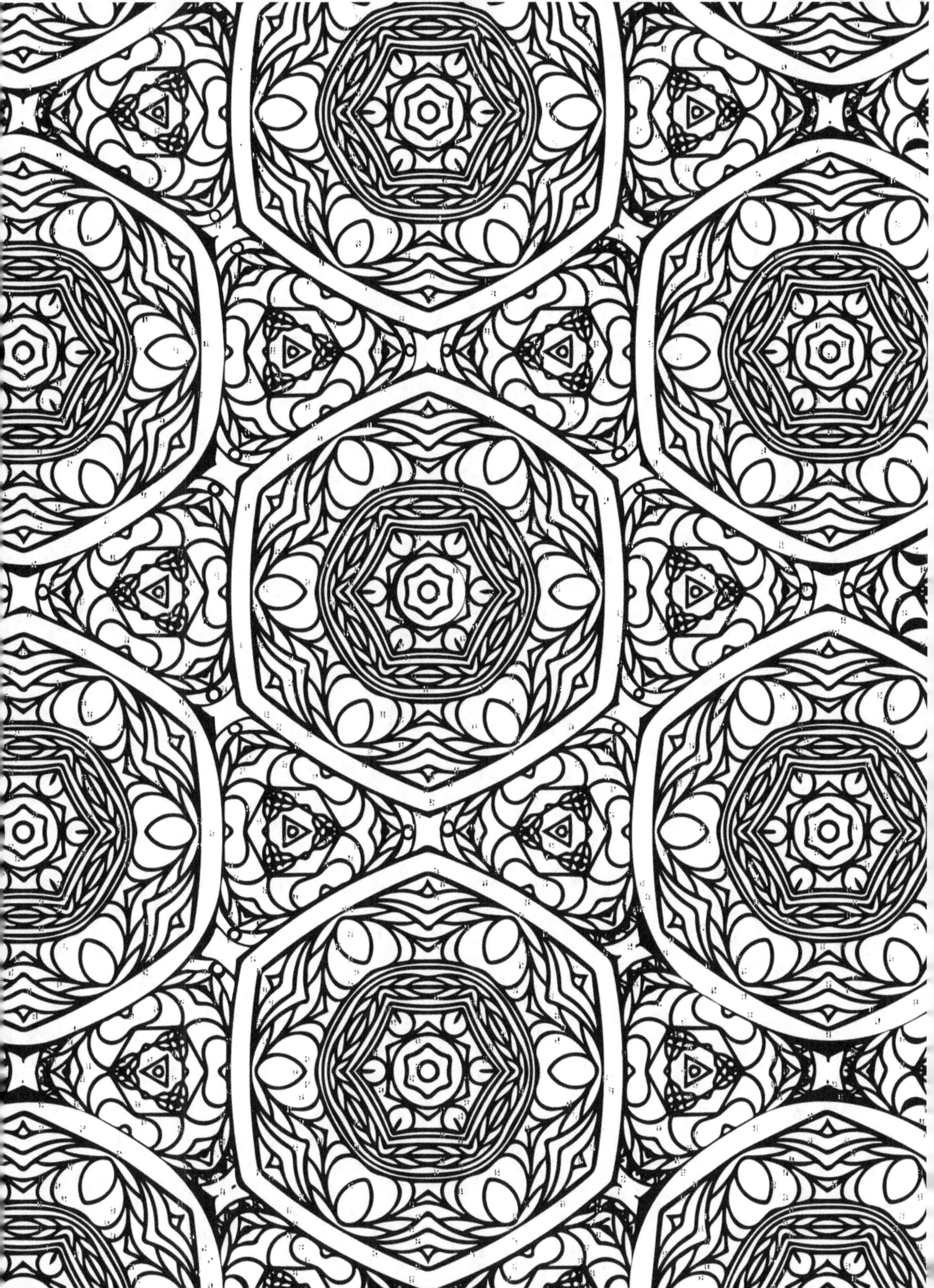

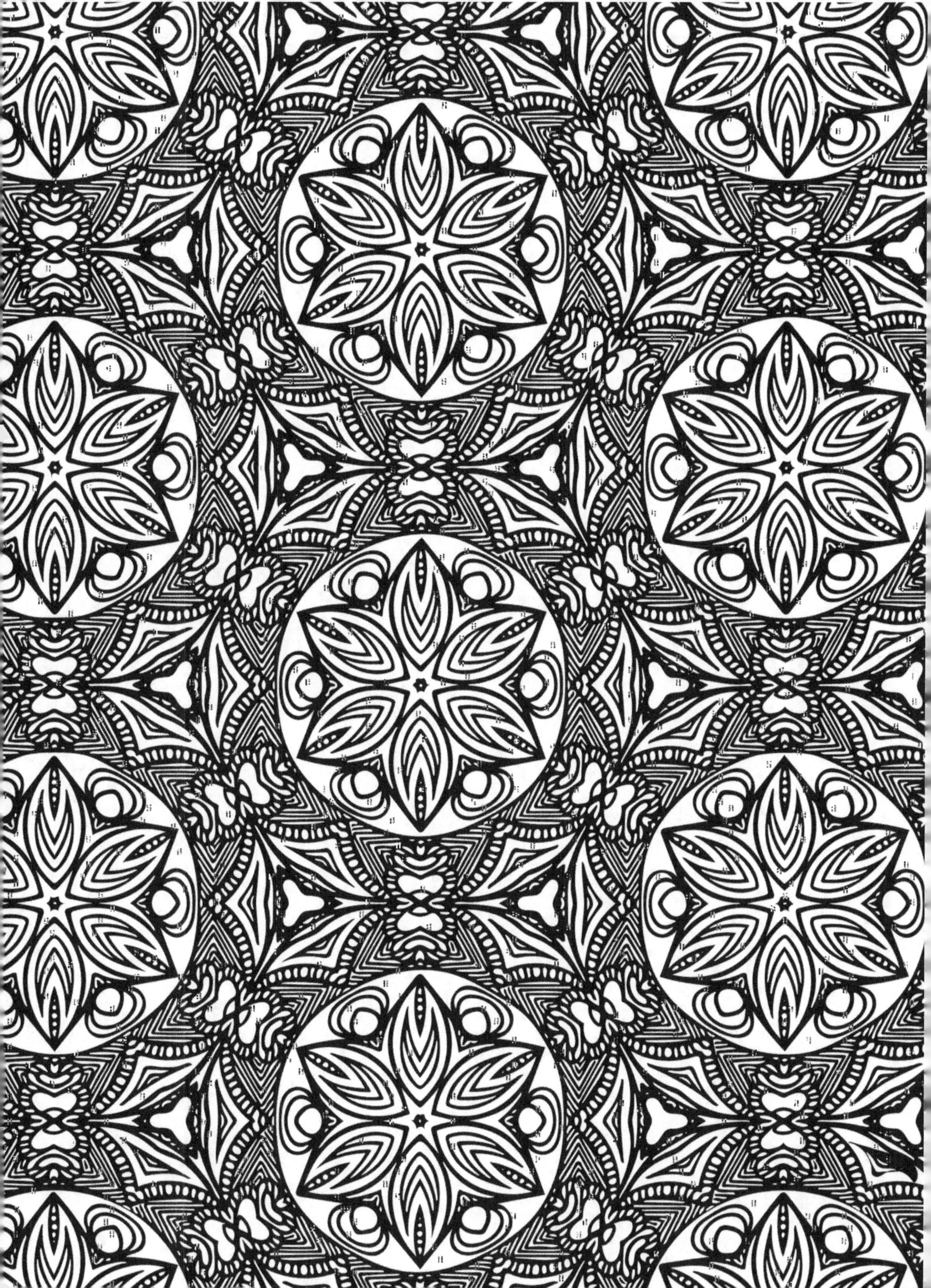

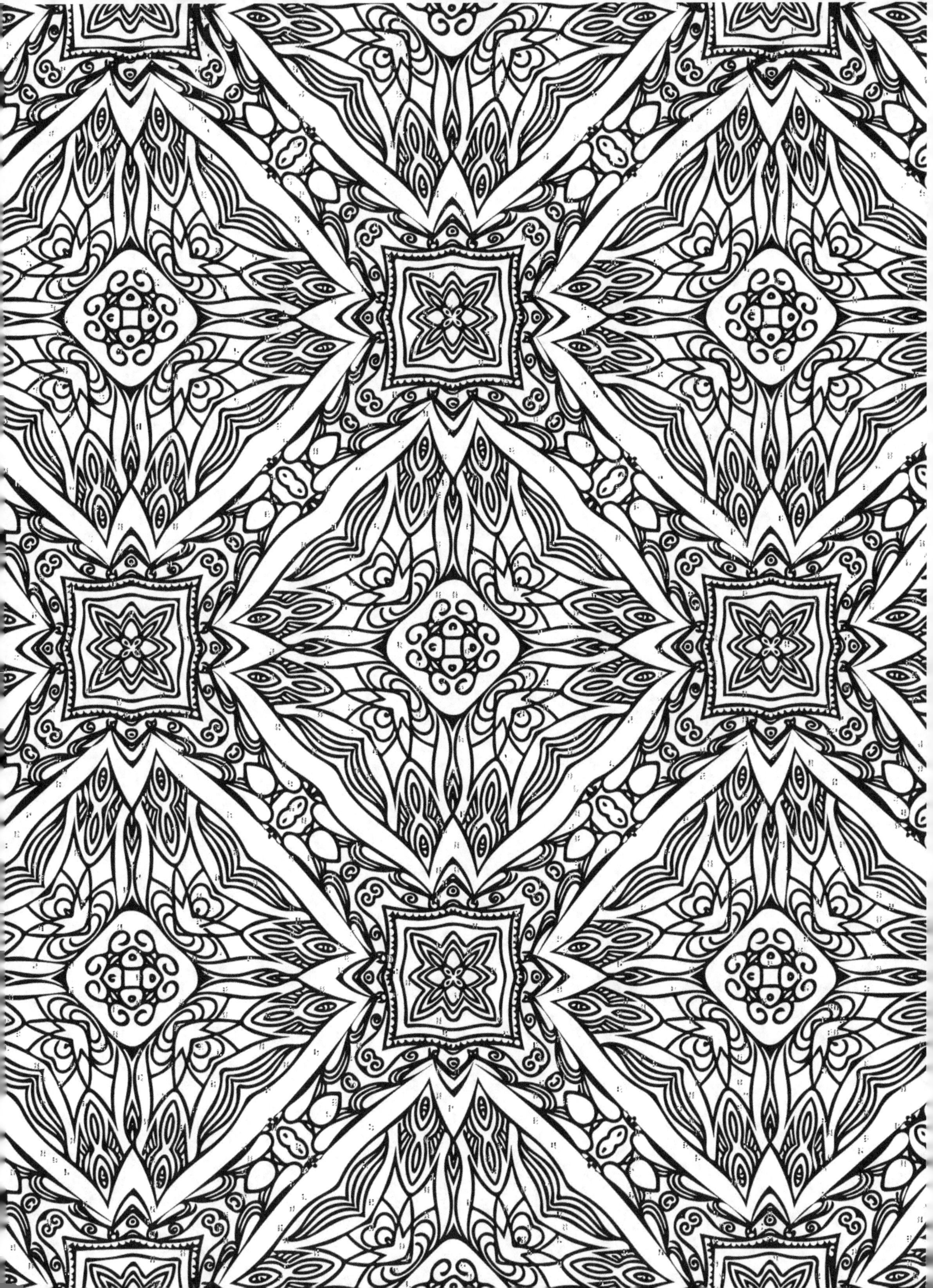

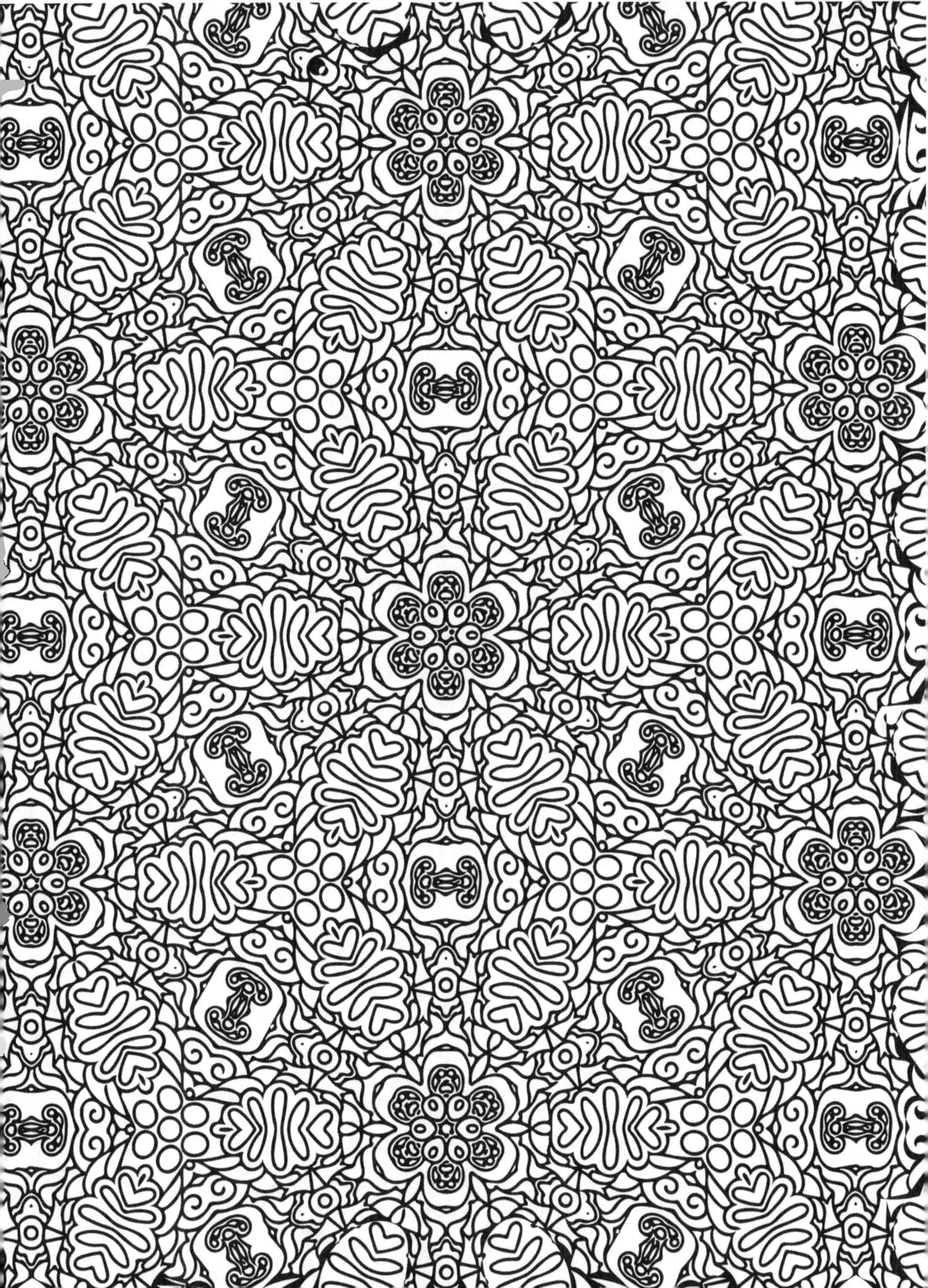

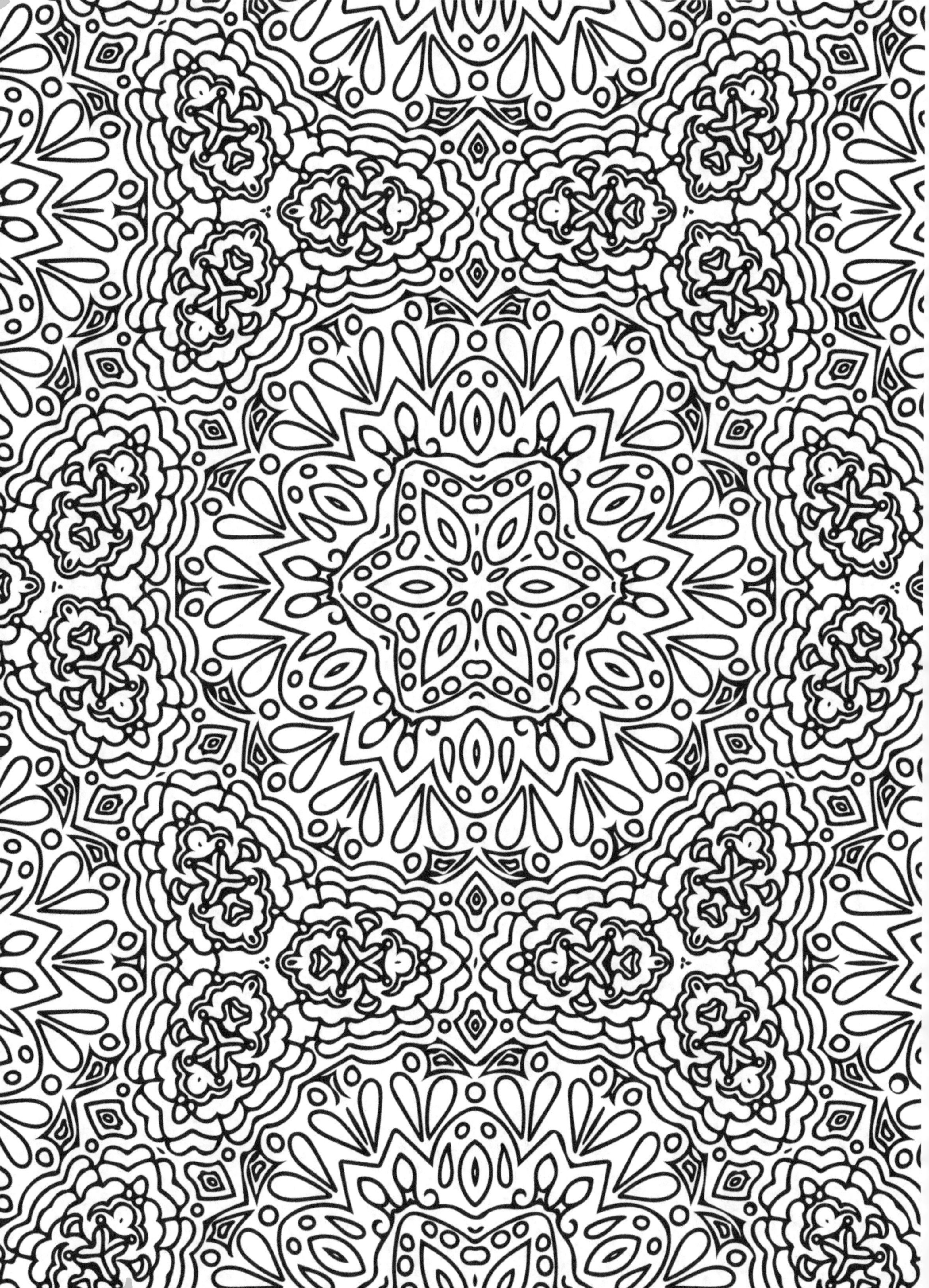

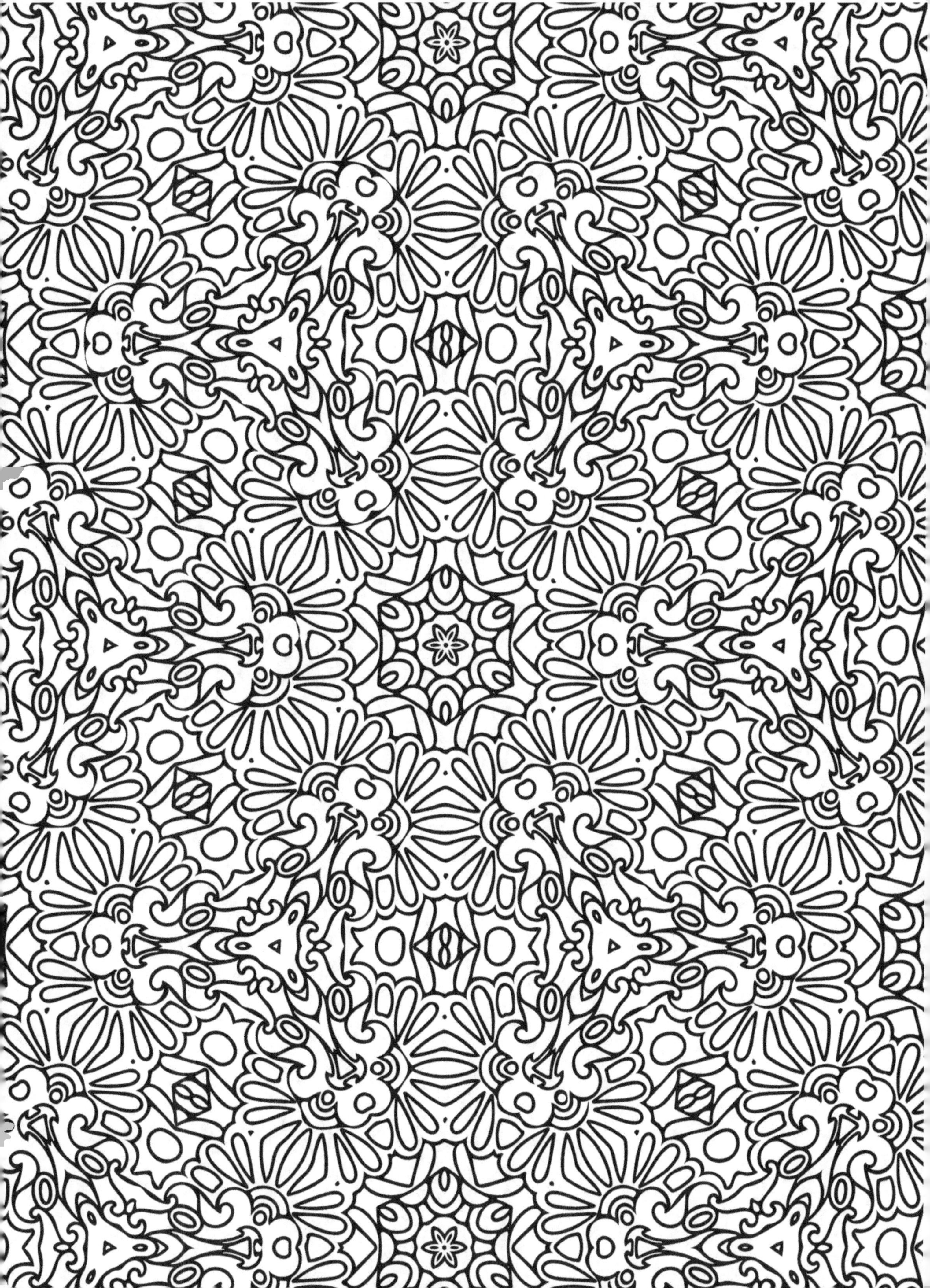

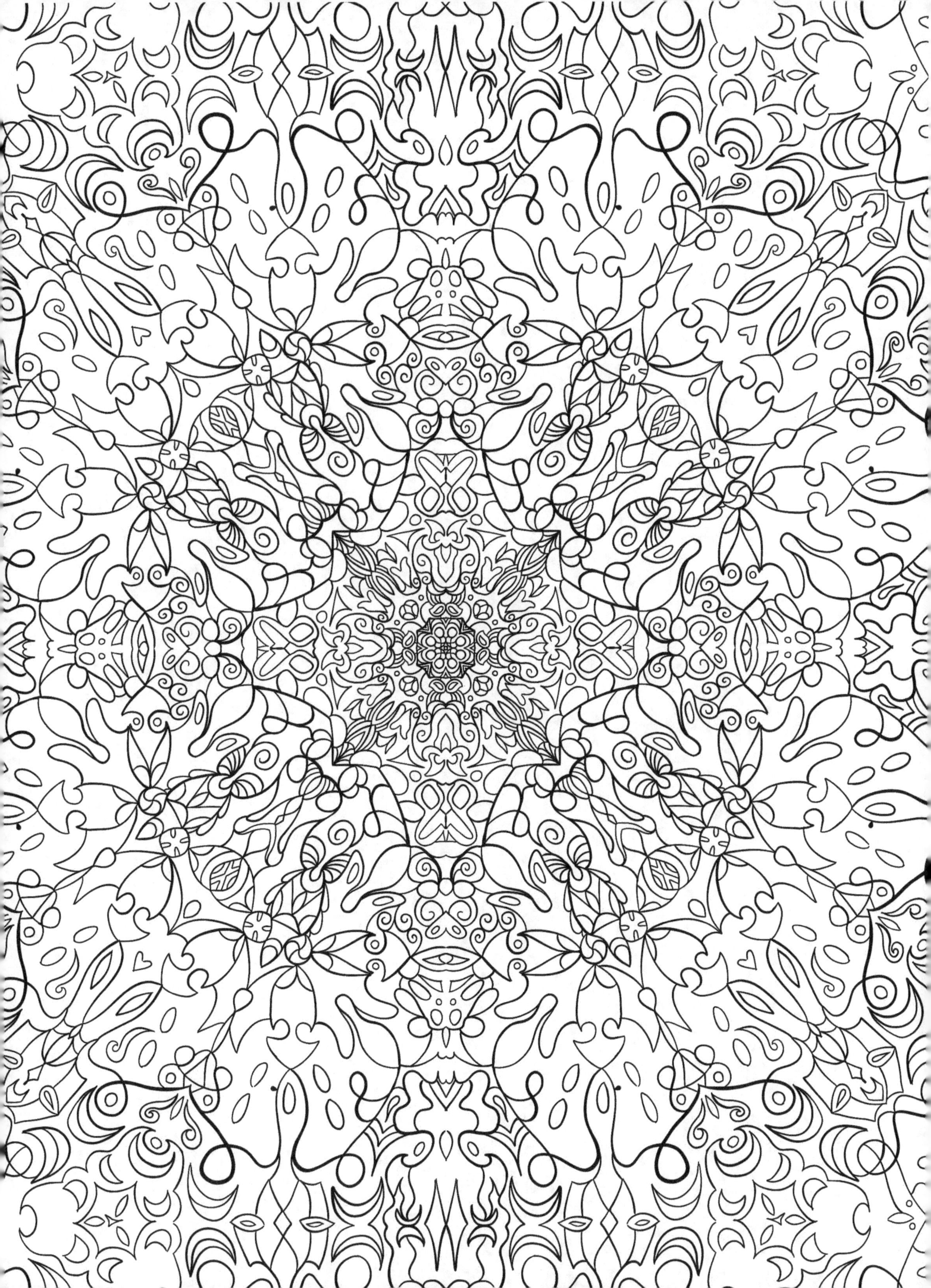

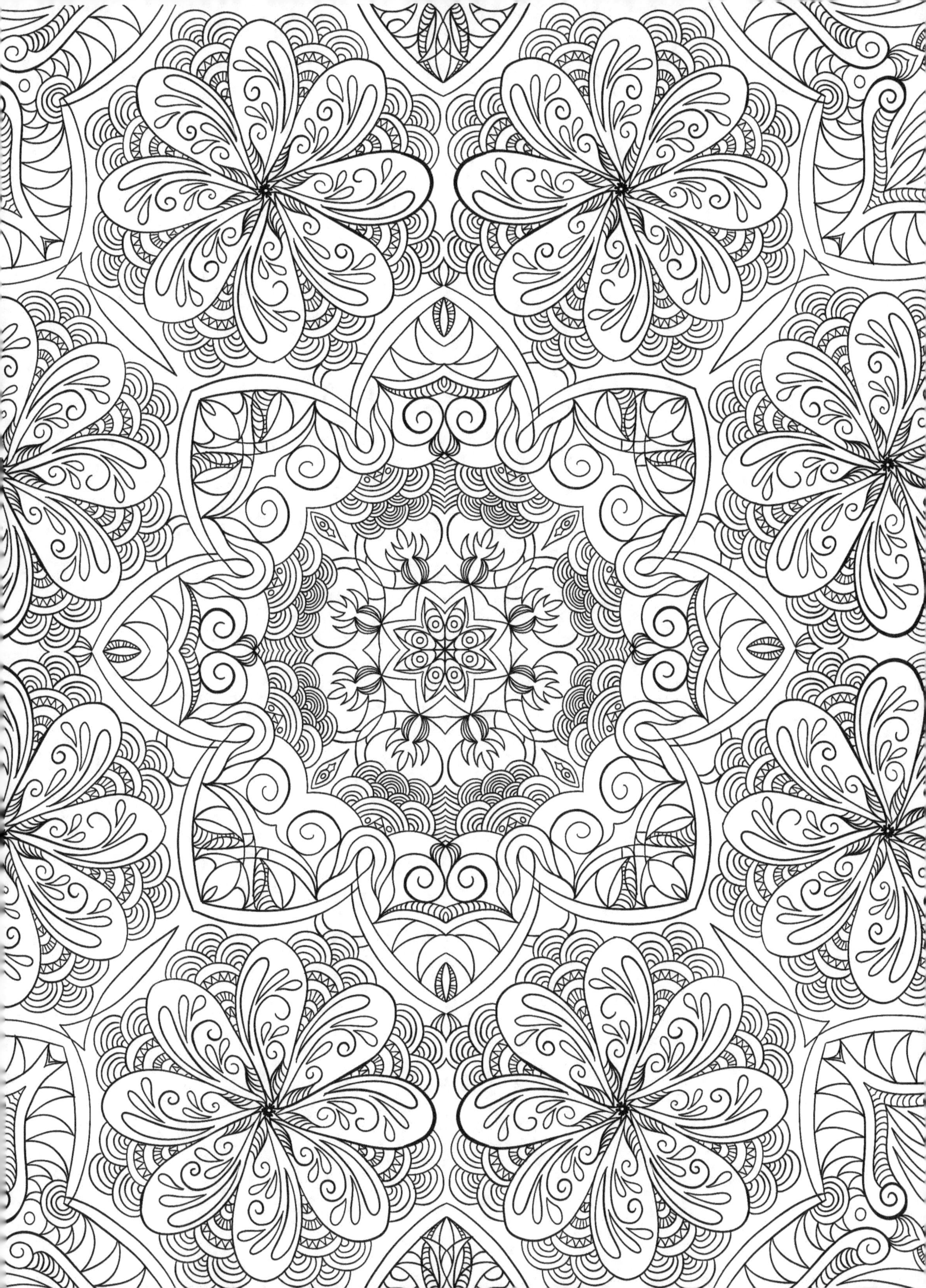

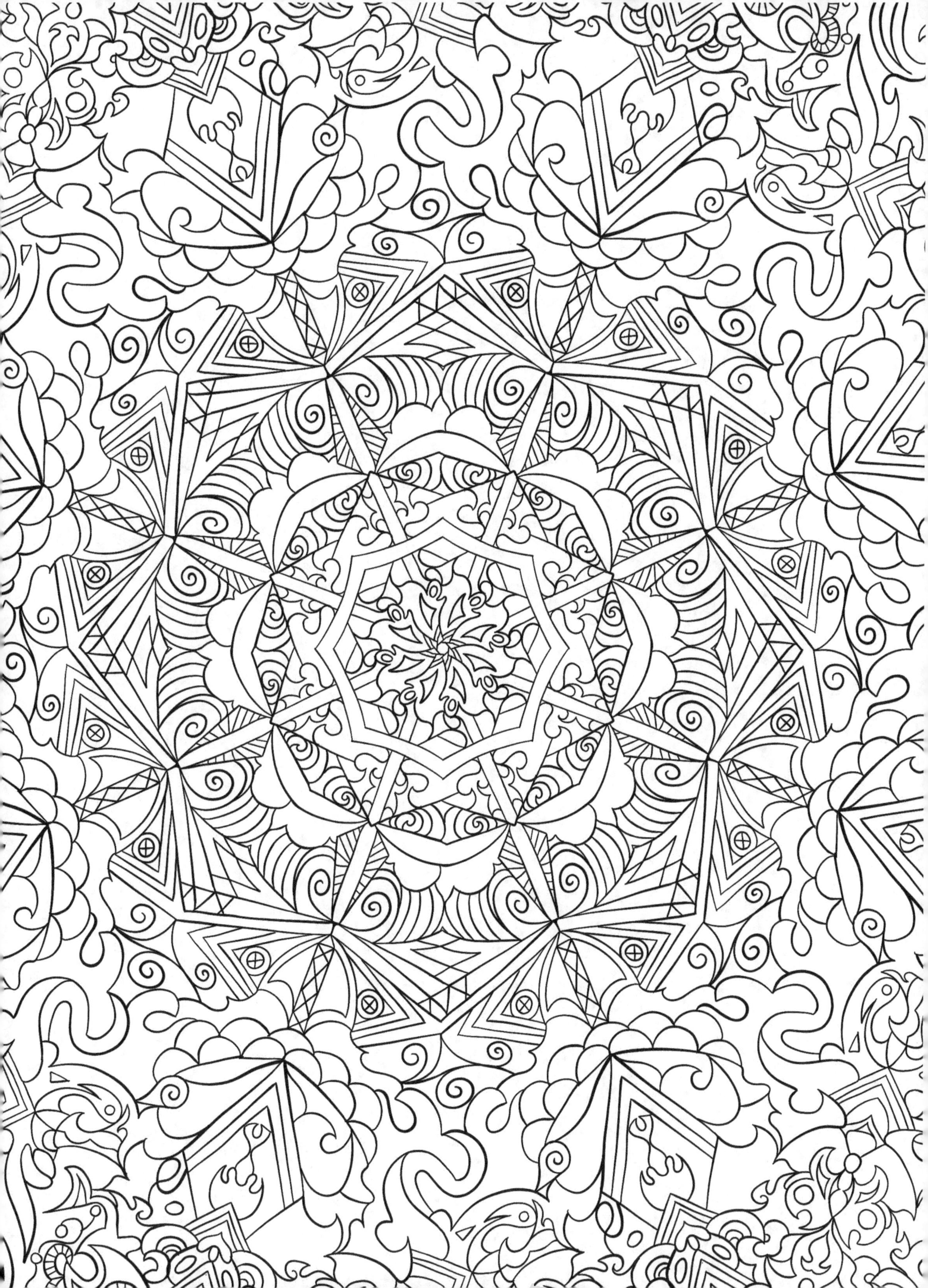

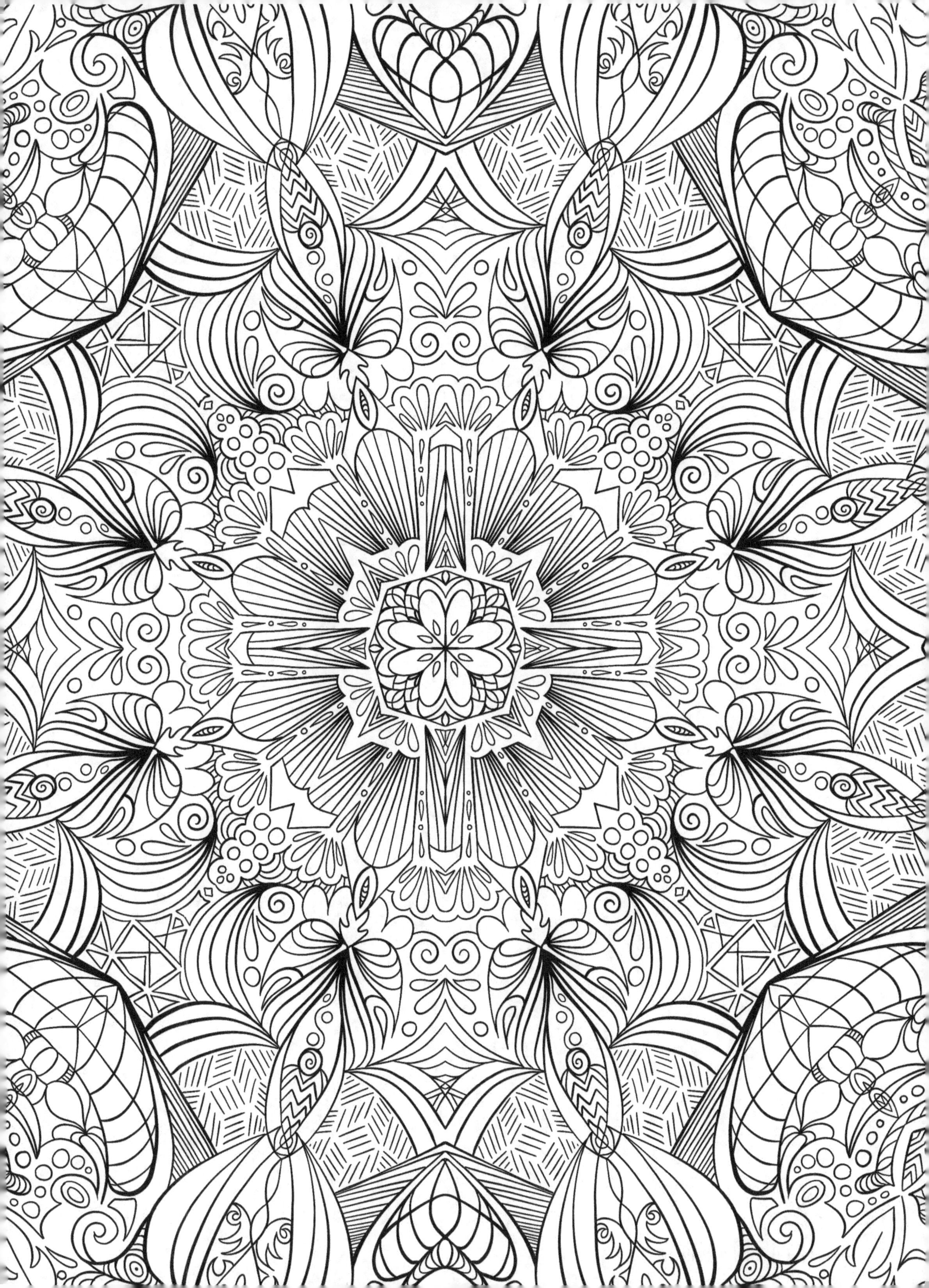

www.ingramcontent.com/pod-product-compliance
Lightning Source LLC
Chambersburg PA
CBHW082246060726
47598CB00017B/2827